HOW TO REMEMBER MUSIC

MUSIC

by David Ash

First published in Great Britain by David Ash,
10 Woodshill Avenue, Rednal, Birmingham B45 8HD.

Also available from the same author:

    HOW TO PLAY MUSIC BY EAR
      (Price £5.00 inc. p&p)

    DON'T SHOOT THE ORGANIST
      (Price £3.25 inc. p&p)

ISBN 0 9509477 1 7

Printed in Great Britain by
Ebenezer Baylis & Son Ltd.,
The Trinity Press, Worcester.

Cover design by Tony James Chance, M.A.

Typed on a Canon AP 300 Electronic Typewriter

Acknowledgements

A big thank you to all the supporters of my first book, HOW TO PLAY MUSIC BY EAR, for the reaction and feedback which has prompted me to write this book. The ability to understand and memorise music would appear to be every musician's ambition.

The initial idea for the book was yours, but the finished article owes much to teamwork — the same team as for book number one:

SUE, my wife, who shouldered my domestic commitments;

TONY JAMES CHANCE, Stourbridge's historical illustrator, part-time battle re-enactor and garret occupant for his splendid cover design;

GERRY KING of Bournemouth, music setter, a genuine and helpful man who advised me on music presentation;

PAUL SAWTELL of Hereford, master musician, for his valued help in proof reading;

...and, performing wonders in translating our ideas into final copy whilst coping with each conceivable problem that could and did arise, the unsung heroine of every book and article, JOYCE SCHOFIELD.

Foreword

The key to progress in music is MEMORY, and in this book, designed specifically for home organists and keyboard players, we invite you to investigate a variety of different approaches. Every reader will have individual needs, abilities, motivation and receptiveness, so if the first approach doesn't seem applicable to you, read on and investigate the next one, as that might just be the one that suits you. The first question to ask yourself is, "<u>Why</u> do I want to memorise music?" and your answer to yourself will give you the goal to aim for and the motivation to succeed.

Once you've laid your foundations by learning to read music and recognise chord symbols, then you start to make progress. However, progress rarely comes as fast as you would like and often the greatest stumbling block to progress is your inability to remember music - even the two or three bars necessary to turn a page in comfort. Once the manuscript is taken away, the shades comes down!

Of course, it is possible to memorise music 'parrot fashion', but it is the wise musician who pauses first to prepare his groundwork. The book stresses the importance of 'understanding' as the main support to memory, and it details techniques of subdividing your pieces into small, self-contained sequences. Once music is set out before you in a consistent and organised way, you will find that fear of the unknown starts to diminish. Start at the Section that suits you best, be it BASIC, INTERMEDIATE or ADVANCED and work through all the tunes in that Section. Against each tune are listed 'recognition' points of special importance for your memory to latch on to, plus points of specific interest which that tune may illustrate.

Often the least considered aspect, but every bit as important as the organisation and preparation of your music, is your organisation of yourself. Before you start on the practical work, you have to learn to harness your mental energies so that you work and memorise efficiently. For this reason you will find that the first chapter is on the psychology of learning and remembering as applied to music, and it is presented as a series of hints and tips relating to MOTIVATION, UNDERSTANDING and COMMONSENSE. Once you start to make practical demands on yourself and begin to experience success and failure, then a re-read of this chapter might be just what you need to eliminate your failures and keep your enthusiasm bubbling. Nothing succeeds like success!

Read through the book and work through the examples, taking it slowly at first, setting your targets low and gradually building on each success. It's a book for 'doing', not just reading, so take it at your own pace and start to enjoy a new dimension in music. Remember the motto, THE KEY TO PROGRESS IN MUSIC IS MEMORY.

Contents

How to use this book

The first item on our agenda is to understand the layout of the book and to do this we must look at the overall picture to see where the boundaries are, and then at what we have to learn within them.

Broadly, the book is split into two halves – THEORY and PRACTICAL – with five theoretical chapters in the first half and 29 practical examples in the second half. Chapter 1, HOW TO HARNESS YOUR MEMORY, is not a learned psychological discourse, but a digest of hints, tips and observations to help you organise your own mental processes and learning techniques. Chapters 2-4, HOW TO REMEMBER MELODY, HOW TO REMEMBER HARMONY and HOW TO REMEMBER MELODY AND HARMONY TOGETHER, are three closely related chapters which are designed to help you prepare your practical approach to memorising music. Only then, in Chapter 5, THEORY REVISION, do we get down to discussing those aspects which are necessary to provide you with sufficient musical knowledge to tackle the PRACTICAL SECTION in a worthwhile manner.

The 29 practical examples are graded progressively to provide a framework for study and are grouped into three sections:

1. BASIC   2. INTERMEDIATE   3. ADVANCED

and within each section, we categorise the tunes as belonging to one of the following groups:

(a) JINGLES
(b) SONGS FOR SPECIAL OCCASIONS
(c) EVERGREENS OR STANDARDS
(d) PARTY OR PRACTICE PIECES

These examples have been selected with two requirements in mind: firstly that they should be familiar and popular, and secondly that they should progressively introduce your memories to new harmonic concepts. Each tune is examined under the following headings:

(1) INFORMATION TO BE REMEMBERED IN ASSOCIATION WITH THE TITLE
(2) HARMONIC PRINCIPLES INVOLVED
(3) MEMORY JOGGERS

It seems sensible, if you are going to devote your time to remembering music, to spend it learning tunes that you will ultimately need to know. In the SONGS FOR SPECIAL OCCASIONS category, therefore, you will find a selection ranging from Birthday to Christmas and Goodnight songs – all 'required' playing material to tuck up your sleeves for an emergency! We progressively introduce new harmonic features and show how they fit into the harmonic 'families' that go towards the composition of all songs. It is stressed throughout the book that memory must come from <u>understanding</u> if it is to be meaningful and lasting, so we analyse the harmonic 'families' you will meet in popular music in the THEORY REVISION chapter so that we can then identify them as they occur in the practical examples.

Although the primary objective throughout is to become efficient in memorising music, you will have the bonus of examining a lot of new theories that will contribute towards your understanding and enjoyment of music.

On the next page you will find a block diagram of the book which will help you to find your way quickly around it, as it is the sort of book where you will need to flip backwards and forwards to refresh your memories and examine concepts for a second and third time as one section reinforces another. Find the memory technique that suits you best, build up a background of fundamental musical knowledge and with these foundations you will make progress that will enhance your enjoyment of music.

Theory

HOW TO:-

<table>
<tr>
<td>

HARNESS
YOUR
MEMORY

Page 3
</td>
<td>

REMEMBER
MELODY

Page 10
</td>
<td>

REMEMBER
HARMONY

Page 21
</td>
<td>

REMEMBER
MELODY
AND
HARMONY
TOGETHER

Page 27
</td>
<td>

THEORY
REVISION

Page 30
</td>
</tr>
</table>

Practical

How to harness your memory

It is everyone's ideal to be able to reproduce music that they have previously played or heard whether it be by a process of practice and understanding or by an intuitive recall. It doesn't really matter how we achieve this objective - the end result justifies whatever mental processes may be necessary. Gifts bestowed by heaven such as photographic memories and perfect pitch are so few and far between that we must align our approach to the subject of MEMORY to allow the average player first to question why he wishes to memorise music, secondly to help him understand the learning and memory processes that are common to everyone and, thirdly, to provide hints and tips on how he may achieve his ambition.

MOTIVATION	UNDERSTANDING YOUR LEARNING AND MEMORY PROCESSES	HINTS & TIPS ON MEMORISING

1. MOTIVATION

People are motivated to wish to improve their memory, and this prompts two observations:

(1) Any person who does wish to improve his memory will do better by understanding his own memory processes and the material he wishes to learn, and

(2) Any success he may have with a 'system' is usually as as result of the stimulus to his thinking rather than the content of the course.

It's a bit like understanding chord construction versus the use of one finger chords on an organ. By the time you've programmed your mind to:

(a) Press the appropriate root note

(b) Press the next black note below it

(c) Maybe press a pedal as well, and

(d) Move your right foot to operate a switch on the swell pedal

all for a minor seventh or whatever, surely it's easier and more sensible to play the chord correctly in the first place!

Once we are motivated to wish to remember music, we must be more specific. It takes self-discipline to stop and analyse why we wish to do things, but if we can just isolate our main objectives, we're better placed to work towards that goal. For instance, do we merely wish to play in a smooth and fluent style or do we wish to know more about our subject? Perhaps we wish to be respected by our colleagues for our amazing ability to be able to play without music or, on the other hand, we might be fighting a battle with ourselves in that we may have a personal target in trying to accurately remember a piece of music. Maybe we have the motivation that comes from positive feedback; we try small passages, setting our targets low at first and, encouraged by our success with these small beginnings, we attempt more ambitious projects. The hurdle here is to get started. Until you make the positive effort to do something for yourself, you are forever in the wilderness. Have a go and then sit back and see what you've achieved. You don't need to set the world on fire but when you do manage to remember something or, alternatively, work something out for yourself, then you have the motivation that lurking within you is a more active mind than ever you would have suspected.

That's how we 'psyche' ourselves up. A creative being is within us waiting to set alight our little musical world. In opposition, we have lack of motivation: tiredness, stress, lack of interest in the subject, daydreams and distractions, too many other hobbies and, worst of all, fear of failure. Just to read a list of these is sufficient to bring them out into the open. We all score seven out of seven at times, but to acknowledge their presence enables us to concentrate our minds on the more positive aspects.

The third section in this chapter - HINTS & TIPS - is inevitably linked in some aspects with our motivations. Tips that increase our motivation are a means of helping us get the best out of ourselves. We build upon success, so if a tip tells us to make our initial target small, then we gradually build on these small achievements. As we proceed, we stop to evaluate our progress, and if it is positive then this again fuels our motivation. We might, for example, have got our performance time for Chopin's MINUTE WALTZ down from 3 minutes to 2¼ minutes - still a long way to go, but a step in the right direction!

Much of our motivation is in how we feel about our chances of success. Do we feel confident and is the target pitched at a realistic level? It is one thing to wish to remember a dazzling piece of music, but if this is so far beyond our ability as to be unrealisable, then it will remain a dream that will never be translated into reality. Start in a small way and this will give you the basis on which to build your ambitions for larger projects.

Whatever the reasons that most inspire and fire you, you can now acknowledge to yourself that you possess the determination to remember music. However, determination without a proper learning strategy is guaranteed to involve you in wasted time and effort, so now study the next two sections to learn how to harness your determination most effectively.

2. <u>UNDERSTANDING YOUR LEARNING AND MEMORY PROCESSES</u>

Not only must you develop an appreciation of these theoretical processes, but you must relate them to the practical situation. We all know the disappointment that comes when we make no progress however hard we seem to try, so let us examine a typical learning chart related to time, to see why this may be so.

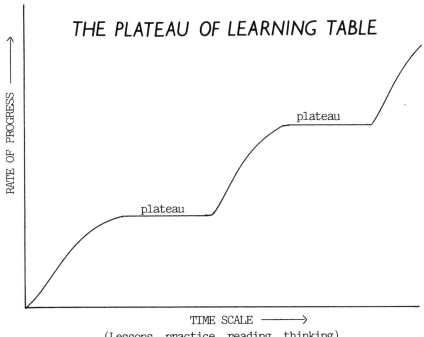

THE PLATEAU OF LEARNING TABLE

RATE OF PROGRESS ⟶

plateau

plateau

TIME SCALE ⟶
(Lessons, practice, reading, thinking)

The graph, often referred to as THE PLATEAU OF LEARNING, is a good visual indication of the sort of progress you are likely to make. You make substantial initial progress as your interest and motivation is sustained, followed by a period of levelling out. That's the time when no matter how hard you practise, you are disappointed that you just cannot make any advancement. The fact that this can be represented diagramatically is sufficient to give you heart because it is apparent that if you persevere, then you will again start to make progress. After a static period, you will start to get those flashes of inspiration when you feel you are beginning to see the 'light'. As the time scale proceeds, you start to reach the upper limit of your natural ability, but that's years away and right now you've just started to climb one of the progress slopes!

Now we have to understand the process by which we can absorb information. Naturally, the hints and tips in the third section are also geared to this, but let us consider here how we can make the most constructive use of our time. The first major concept we have to appreciate is that we possess both a Short Term Memory (STM) and a Long Term Memory (LTM). Whereas the LTM is a vast storehouse of knowledge which may be considered limitless, the STM is exactly the opposite. Before we can absorb musical facts and information into the LTM, they have to be processed in the STM and if the conditions for the transference of information are not right, then we may struggle for hours to no avail. We can best appreciate this by considering, as an example, telephone numbers. Your own number and those of friends you phone often spring immediately to mind, but a telephone number you look up in the directory for a casual call will remain with you until the number is dialled, and then be forgotten. Unless you make the effort to remember the casual number by recitation or redialling several times, then it will disappear from your memory. Imagine the amount of raw material you can assimilate to be less than 10 facts, then you can see that you must be precise in both evaluating the information you wish to learn, and in the manner in which you present it to your memory.

LONG TERM AND SHORT TERM MEMORIES

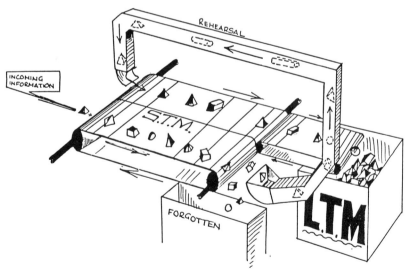

Diagrams are always helpful for us to focus on the points we wish to understand as they provide that additional visual input. Based on the diagram, it will be obvious that we can suggest hints and tips such as:

(1) Information must be presented to your brain in small quantities.

(2) There is a time scale that says you cannot absorb unlimited information in any one period.

(3) Trying to absorb too much new information knocks out that which you have previously half-learned.

We can see now that there is an interaction between motivation and understanding. If you set your targets low, then you have the facility to transfer the information into your LTM store whence it can be retrieved as necessary to provide the foundation for further projects. Once you understand this, your motivation is not based on a vague desire, but on an attainable ambition.

The principle on which many advertisers of memory courses base their product is that of association, (one is the sun, two is blue, three is a bee and so on). To remember a series of numbers you then construct a mental image to represent the number, so that a blue bee flying upwards towards the sun would represent the figure 231. Undoubtedly this may help some people where the facts they wish to remember are unrelated, but in music you must learn to understand logical relationships based on musical principles. Although, as we have stressed, memory must come to a large extent from understanding, until that understanding becomes complete, there are other devices which can help our memories. One of these is the use of mnemonics.

Mnemonics are devices to assist your memory until such time as use and repetition makes recognition automatic. When first learning the notes on the treble clef, we use the mnemonic FACE for the notes falling in the spaces and Every Good Boy Deserves Favour for the notes falling on the lines. When you need to remember the sequence of chords lying in the segment of the cycle of fifths clockwise from C (see page 38), you may refer to Alsatian Dogs Growl at Cats to represent A7 to D7 to G7 to C or, if you want to go round all twelve keys of the cycle starting at C, you may use Can Fried Bacon Eggs And Dumplings Give Boys Extra Appetite During Games? These, then, are mnemonics and they can be of great help in many avenues of study.

Whilst mnemonics may help with the initial learning stages, it is essential, in order to get more benefit from our learning/memory capacity, to understand the basic material we wish to learn. Individual passages and overall concepts cannot necessarily be understood until we arrange and present the information to our brains in a logical and sequential format. We must organise the material in smaller, self-contained sections so that we are aware of overall 'form' and 'shape'. We must join those sections that we don't understand to those that we do, so that their inter-relationship may be observed. Music is the product of a creative mind and our preference for a particular piece may be because of its sheer freshness. Paradoxically, it may be because it is fresh and unique that we cannot predict or understand it. However, we do have to develop a familiarity with musical principles, sequences and relationships so that if we wish to remember the piece we may do so on the basis of understanding. This all takes time and needs a broad base of musical foundations and principles to which to refer and with which to compare: not necessarily a subject for progressive study, but one of gradual assimilation.

Finding our own best learning processes is often as a result of identifying with particular hints and tips that seem to work for us. These learning strategies are acquired and we adapt them to different situations because one approach may work for one type of material and a different approach may be necessary for another type of material. We come to realise that we are most receptive to new material at certain times of the day: for some people this is early morning and for others, late at night. On the one hand you may find yourself alert in the morning, and on the other hand you may subscribe to the theory that information you learn last thing at night is digested in your sub-conscious so that you may recall your evening's studies perfectly the next morning. This sort of evaluation is made by trial and error and the hints and tips in the next section will help you to maximise your potential. Possibly the best single piece of advice is to understand, as far as possible, the material which you are attempting to learn and to make it accurate since you will then be able to recall the information in its relevant place. Here is the hard-hitting converse: RUBBISH LEARNED = RUBBISH REMEMBERED.

3. HINTS AND TIPS ON MEMORISING

(a) Based on Motivation

1. Motivation affects learning and memorising, so "Do what you like, and like what you do".

2. Be motivated: build on the success that comes with memorising small amounts of information at a time.

3. Disappointment is anti-motivational.

4. Pick out the interesting bits first - you then have a base to work from.

5. Identify what you would <u>like</u> to do. What is your aim?

6. Don't develop your interest in isolation; relate to your colleagues and nurture that competitive instinct.

7. Read more books on the subject, maybe on the development of music or the composers - anything to increase background knowledge and interest.

8. Identify yourself with a star performer. How does he interpret your favourite tunes, what is it about his style that you like?

9. Consider your chance of success. Do you feel confident that you will achieve success?

10. Evaluate your progress. Have you got the MINUTE WALTZ down to 2½ minutes yet?

(b) Based on Understanding

1. We have a Short Term Memory and a Long Term Memory. Whereas the LTM is virtually limitless, the STM can store only a restricted amount of information - possibly less than 10 facts at a time.

2. We must understand our best methods of transference from STM to LTM:
   * Learn a small amount at a time.
   * Rehearse/recite/practise these items until they are remembered permanently.
   * If necessary, <u>overlearn</u>, i.e. continue to practise even though you have achieved 100% recall.
   * Do not try to learn too many things together - one knocks out the other.
   * Don't overload your STM but have a break of 5 minutes every 15 to 20 minutes.
   * Playing a piece 50 times is not learning. Think about it, rehearse it, practise it.

3. As you will see in the chapter on HOW TO REMEMBER MELODY, review/rehearsal is <u>the</u> most important link in the memory chain. You <u>must</u> rehearse the material you have freshly learned to imprint it indelibly on your memory.

4. You cannot maintain progress indefinitely. Refer to the PLATEAU OF LEARNING TABLE to see that stagnant periods are inevitable.

5. Organise your material into small sections and, if necessary, use mnemonics to help you recall a sequence. Organise your music in a logical way that makes sense.

6. Be aware that the total process involves learning, storage in LTM, and retrieval of information as needed. The more background you acquire, and the more incidental information you absorb, the easier it is to retrieve the material from the LTM. (You will have heard of the 'tip of the tongue' phenomenon where all that is needed is a 'hook of association' to pull the required information from the LTM.)

7. Learn with meaning. Be accurate and understand what you learn. If you learn gibberish and inaccurate data, then that is what is stored in your memory.

8. Have a break every so often for a period of consolidation so that your brain can shed irrelevancies. A rest or a holiday can be beneficial; have you noticed how often you play better when you return from holiday, or on a Monday?

9. Learning receptiveness goes in cycles so discover your best time of day and avoid struggling when you are tired and under stress.

10. Your learning is not necessarily predictable, so try approaching each problem from different angles.

11. Link up new work to old so that the material to be remembered is not viewed in isolation.

12. Make sure there is no ambiguity or sloppiness. Be accurate.

(c) <u>General Hints and Tips</u>

1. Learn with meaning. Have you ever tried learning the pronunciation of a foreign language? Repetition of word sounds is difficult and abstract unless you understand the meaning of the words you are using. So it is with music. Use the pointers in this book to help you understand your music and then you will quickly assimilate new material because... you are 'learning with meaning'. The easy way out for a lot of people is to learn through repetition because it takes less effort of will.

2. If you haven't got technique, it doesn't matter what's in your head, you will be unable to express it musically. Remember that favourite adage, 'Technique is half in the head and half in the hands'. Develop your technique by whatever device you can and all of a sudden you will find that you will derive great pleasure from playing scales, arpeggios and other exercises. When you translate these skills into expressing yourself creatively, your music will take on new meaning.

3. Don't overload your brain.

4. Give the difficult bits extra attention until they are fluent. If you falter at a complex bit regularly, then this is stored in your memory as part of the tune! Similarly your memory does not distinguish between good and bad habits, so feed in good and accurate habits in the first place.

5. Your learning is greatly accelerated by imitating a skilled performer. Observe the points you identify with in your teacher or your colleagues, or even on records.

6. Avoid linear learning. This is where you play your next notes in relation to the current ones and if you break one link in the chain you are lost. Far better to understand the underlying principles so that your mind can assist the muscular memory present in your fingers. Imagine your fingers remembering the tune for you and then being asked to change key!

7. When you study, the conditions under which you study have a significant bearing on your results. Avoid distractions, ensure there's adequate lighting and that the atmosphere is not stuffy.

8. Learn all facts properly and don't be lazy or 'fudge' the chords. Make sure there is no ambiguity in your harmonies. Is it Dm7 or F6?

9. One tip from a classical teacher was that to play a piece at exactly half speed was a good precursor to a concert performance since your fingers had to be accurate and precise and the speed multiple, times 2, was felt naturally.

10. Everyone makes progress for different reasons, so an approach that may be fruitful for one person might not necessarily be so for another. The moral is, TRY DIFFERENT

APPROACHES. Everyone has heard of the phrase, 'Let's look at things from a different angle', and this merely paraphrases the point. Find the approaches that have meaning for you and persevere with them, although you must be flexible since rigid learning strategies may not always be appropriate. Do an Edward De Bono on your music and turn it inside out until you find out what makes both you and your music tick.

11. It's not only your fingers that you need to flex. We have all played Japanese instruments at some time or another, so let's take a leaf out of their book to promote some mental well-being. Did you ever see that T.V. programme where the Japanese car workers limbered up before their day's graft? Well, we too have to be in good physical condition before our mental processes can get into top gear. Extra helpings of plum duff and four pints of best bitter are definitely not conducive to brainstorms so, if you want to prove a point, do half-a-dozen press-ups first just to see for yourselves how it livens up your minds!

HAPPY PLAYING

How to remember melody

In order to memorise we must organise, and the first thing to organise is our approach to remembering melody. We need to keep in mind the 'thread' of our approach so that we can see what has to be done as groundwork, then once these foundations are laid, we can build on them and apply ourselves to the specific area of melody.

We will therefore sub-divide our overall approach as follows:

MEMORISING MELODIC INTERVALS	DEVELOPMENT OF RELATIVE PITCH	MELODY ORGANISATION PROCEDURES	TABULATION OF HINTS & TIPS

Hints and tips are fascinating and very much like reading horoscopes. There will always be something that you, individually, can identify with. However, when it comes to memorising, no amount of reading can take the place of solid musical background, and for this reason the development of your 'ear' for melody is essential. In order to recall music accurately you need to be able to draw on a variety of musical resources. These resources can take the form of harmonic knowledge and anticipation, a muscular memory whereby your fingers instinctively move to the correct notes, maybe a visual recall of some of the music whereby you can picture the notes on the stave, an awareness of melody notes compatible with familiar chords, etc, etc. The combination of approaches you take to reproduce your music is individual to you, but it is important to be able to get back to first principles so that you can work out which notes are required if your memory processes falter.

1. MEMORISING MELODIC INTERVALS

The intervals illustrated below are those commonly encountered within the span of one octave. You've probably looked at them and played them hundreds of times, but have you ever stopped to 'listen' to them? Now that you will no longer have the music in front of you, you need to learn the 'sound' of them, and these 'interval mnemonics' will help, and can be used as a cross-reference to fix the sounds of the intervals in your mind.

This may possibly be the first occasion on which you have questioned the very existence of intervals. Start thinking of melodies as 'scale' or 'arpeggio' type, and ask yourself whether each successive note sticks closely to its neighbour (scale type) or leaps about as in A DAY TRIP TO BANGOR and UP A LAZY RIVER (arpeggio type). Successive movements between melody notes are all intervals, but stop to consider whether the interval is large or small and start to develop accuracy in reproducing each leap. You may remember the actual notes themselves, or you may start to remember the sound of the interval by cross-reference to the mnemonics or other examples, or you may support your memory processes (should they falter) by developing your sense of 'relative pitch' which will enable you to predict the second note by reference to the first. Throughout the book, do make it a policy to stop, take stock, and consider different approaches.

2. DEVELOPMENT OF RELATIVE PITCH

What is a key? A key, and the melodies and harmonies performed in that key, are all bound together in a common relationship to a single note, the key note or tonic. Consider the key note to be the stable, foundation note and you will start to appreciate that at any part of the tune your melody and harmony are not to be considered in isolation, but in relation to the stable tonic key note. Keys may change in pitch, and the scales based upon key notes may differ (major, minor, etc.) but once the initial 'home' key is established, all subsequent melodies and harmonies possess an identity relative to the key/tonic note.

Now that we've investigated the written intervals so that we can store their 'sounds' in our memories as reference examples, let us consider an alternative approach where the interval exists solely in our head and we have to develop a method to accurately identify and reproduce it. Not 'pure' memory this time, but essential as a back-up system if our memory deserts us. Let's set about working out the intervals for ourselves. (Not only is this approach valid for melody support, but you will find it of enormous help later when it comes to identifying harmonies.)

Consider first a major scale of C:

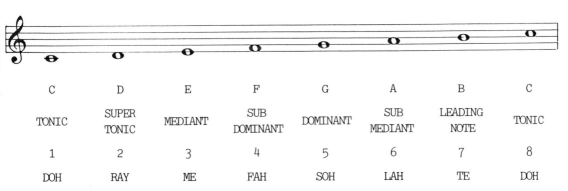

C	D	E	F	G	A	B	C
TONIC	SUPER TONIC	MEDIANT	SUB DOMINANT	DOMINANT	SUB MEDIANT	LEADING NOTE	TONIC
1	2	3	4	5	6	7	8
DOH	RAY	ME	FAH	SOH	LAH	TE	DOH

However you think of this scale and however you remember it doesn't matter, it is the awareness of each note in relation to the key note/tonic/root of C that is important. For our study purposes, let's refer to degrees of the scale, 1 to 8, tonic C (1) to upper tonic C (8). Sing the major scale first to yourself and check your accuracy against the keyboard – if you play wrong notes and can <u>hear</u> that they are wrong, then this means your sense of pitch is all right. Let's now simplify the scale by singing just the significant notes of the key chord C in arpeggio form, C E G C, which you may also now sing as 1 3 5 8. That's great so far, so now fill in the gaps by singing each segment like this, 1 2 3, 3 2 1 and then 3 4 5, 5 4 3 and so on. Notice how it is preferable to sing numbers rather than notes from the scale as by this method numbers can apply to any chosen key/scale.

When you do wish to anchor everything down, you may think, "Yes, I remember, I play SPANISH EYES in the key of G, but what on earth is the starting note?" and the development of your sense of relative pitch quickly tells you that you start on the 3rd degree of the scale, in the key of G, a B note. You may easily consolidate this approach by experimenting with the starting notes in the Practical Section where you have the 'answers' written in, so that you can check your accuracy.

Now let's list seven tunes, each starting on a different degree of the scale and in each one, use the technique detailed above to confirm that each starting, or lead-in note, is precisely that stated. Use your ears to move to whichever tonic is most comfortable/closest, i.e. either count down to 1 or up to 8 and learn to take short cuts, e.g. for the waltz ALWAYS, either count down 5 3 1 to the lower tonic note, or up 5 6 7 8 to get to the upper tonic. Here's the list:

TITLE	DEGREE OF SCALE	FIRST WORD	'COUNT' TO THE TONIC
THE NATIONAL ANTHEM	Starts on the tonic	"God.."	-
YESTERDAY	" " " second	"Yesterday.."	2 1
SPANISH EYES	" " " third	"Blue.."	3 2 1
BRIDGE OVER TROUBLED WATER	" " " fourth	"When.."	4 3 2 1
HAPPY BIRTHDAY TO YOU	" " " fifth	"Happy..."	5 3 1
MOONLIGHT IN VERMONT	" " " sixth	"Pennies.."	6 7 8
BY THE TIME I GET TO PHOENIX	" " " seventh	"By.."	7 8

In the Practical Section you'll see the tunes you are going to learn to memorise, so go through them now to determine their starting notes and see how you fare. It will come quite naturally to you to remember the titles of tunes and their associated keys, but you will not remember their starting notes so easily, so this method will give your memories that little bit of assistance so necessary for maintaining confidence. And even if you think you can remember the starting notes, what about all those tunes that have 'lead-in' notes before you meet the double bar lines at the actual start of the tune? Although it's 'visually' satisfying to consider the starting note as the note that falls on beat 1 of the first bar, the starting note or notes are really the opening words of the lyric, irrespective of where they fall, although in instrumentals (i.e. no lyrics), we would normally call them lead-in notes or anacrusis. (BY THE TIME I GET TO PHOENIX has 2 notes prior to the double bar lines whilst Phil Spector's RIVER DEEP, MOUNTAIN HIGH bounces in with a full bar and a half of lead-in.) This method of singing 'scale notes' and 'arpeggio notes' to identify intervals in relation to the tonic as a support to your other memory processes is not just confined in its application to starting notes, but can be used throughout the song whenever you feel unsure of your bearings and your memory seems to be faltering.

3. MELODY ORGANISATION PROCEDURES

Five pages of sheet music complete with introduction, verse, repeats and key changes are enough to deter even the most ambitious student because of the sheer volume of information. However, once we start to scythe through the repeats, ignore the key changes and rewrite the melody with chord symbols above, thus avoiding bass clef, we can then see the wood from the trees. Let's consider the construction of popular songs. Typically, we may start with a verse or an introduction before the chorus (or refrain). Often the verse may be obscure or absent altogether and only the more popular chorus section will be played, in which case it is up to us to organise it into a more easily remembered and understood 'visual' layout.

The first thing to appreciate is that tunes are nearly always constructed of multiples of 4 bars. Visual presentation is important in that the similarities, repeats, unexpected twists and turns, etc. that we take for granted in our listening, become significant and clearly visible when reproduced in a '4 bars to the line' format, starting with bar 1 to the left-hand margin. How often on the printed copy you find an extended introduction resulting in the chorus starting half way across the page! When this happens, small regular features that would otherwise be apparent are obscured.

Having established that the sub-divisions are normally of 4 bars duration, what of the larger divisions? You must develop your study of your favourite pieces to ascertain whether the format is two 16 bar passages, a series of 12 bar passages, or some other combination. It will help you to observe how the music is displayed in the Practical Section later in the book. Be aware that the standard composition of many evergreens is an AABA format, where the initial 8 bar Section A repeats, followed by a Middle 8 Section B and finally a repeat of Theme A. (It is as well to point out at this early stage that nearly always the tonality of Section B differs from Section A, i.e. a change of key is implied but not actually written in as such.) You will see many other types of format when you reach the Practical Section, and so that these are brought immediately to your attention, we preface each example by a grid so that the salient features of the structure of the tune are easily absorbed.

TYPICAL GRID ACCOMPANYING PRACTICAL EXAMPLES

STRUCTURE				
WRITTEN KEY	STARTING/LEAD-IN NOTE	CHORD	TEMPO/RHYTHM	ORGANISATION OF SECTIONS

TYPICAL AABA FORMAT

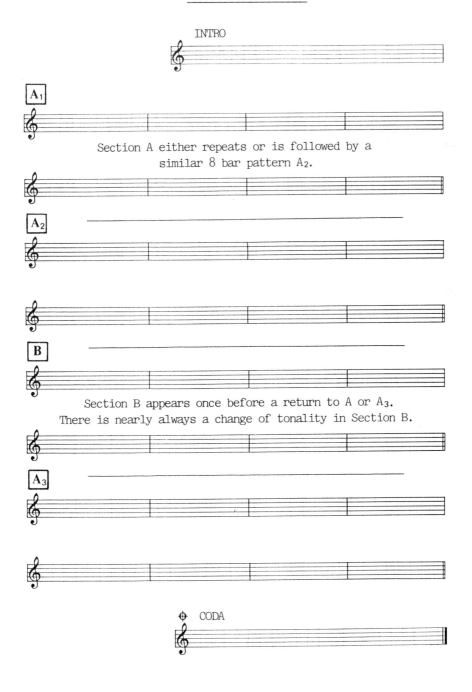

INTRO

A₁

Section A either repeats or is followed by a similar 8 bar pattern A₂.

A₂

B

Section B appears once before a return to A or A₃.
There is nearly always a change of tonality in Section B.

A₃

⊕ CODA

14

TITLE	SECTION LENGTH	FORMAT
AROUND THE WORLD	2x16 BARS	
LOVE ME TENDER	2x8 BARS	A B
SPANISH EYES	2x16 BARS	
HONEYSUCKLE ROSE	4x8 BARS	
QUANDO QUANDO	4x16 BARS	A A B A
MOONLIGHT SERENADE	3x12 + 1x8 BARS	
SEPTEMBER SONG	4x8 BARS	$A_1 A_2 B A_3$
THE ANNIVERSARY WALTZ	4x8 BARS	
TEA FOR TWO	4x8 BARS	$A_1 B A_2 C$
THE CHARLESTON	4x8 BARS	
I BELIEVE	4x12 BARS	A B A C
I DO LIKE TO BE BESIDE THE SEASIDE	4x8 BARS	

How can we use this organised approach to help our memories? The tune now has a 'visual' structure and together, sight and sound are powerful approaches for our memories to retain the necessary information. Keep the 'blank' format diagram in mind, and referring to the Practical Examples, notice how:

1. We've condensed each tune from many pages and, in so doing, we can focus upon significant parts.
2. We have arranged our melody into Sections A B and so on and have further arranged them into 4 bar patterns that are in line.
3. We can now observe similarities in timing, phrasing and repetition, e.g. timing, phrasing and rests will have a regular pattern, and repeated phrases will spring immediately to our attention (e.g. lines 1 and 3 will often be identical, as will lines 2 and 4, etc.)
4. Lead-in notes, introductions, bridge passages and codas will normally be written away from the main body of the tune and will be remembered for their necessary contribution rather than unsettling the eye with confusing detail.
5. The condensed format allows us to approach the question of dynamics - phrasing, climax, diminuendo, etc. - all factors that contribute to the 'life' and inter- pretation of the piece. It's not just the bare notes of the melody that we need to remember, but also the 'shape' and 'form' of the whole tune - "It's not what you play, but the way that you play it".

These, then, are five benefits arising from the reorganisation of your music, but the greatest single benefit will be derived from making the effort to rewrite the music on to manuscript paper yourself. It is only when you come to do this that you recognise in just which areas your musical understanding is 'shaky' and incomplete. Your first efforts are bound to be slow, but before long you will have the experience behind you that will enable you to reorganise your music mentally, without recourse to felt-tip pens and manuscript. That will be when your memory itself is organised into accepting the salient points that you feed into it. The methods by which you may best do this are covered in the first chapter where we give pointers based on the theory of memory processes.

4. HINTS AND TIPS

Some of these will ring a bell straight away and others will become significant only after you have attempted the Practical Examples. This section is divided into Practical Hints and General Hints applicable to memorising melody. If you feel that some of these pointers have meaning for you, put a tick by them - that will ensure that you are reading in depth rather than skimming over the points made.

Practical Hints for Memory and Recall

1. TIMING = WORDS

This assumes that you already know the pitch of the note, but melody on its own is incomplete without the correct time value of each note. The most useful tip here is to make yourself acquainted with the lyrics to develop timing and that essential sense of dynamics. Timing will often vary during repeats, following the dictate of the lyrics, so this is why a knowledge of the lyric is so important for accurate melody recall. You are excused in the case of virtuoso instrumental numbers and rugby songs! (Please note that in the Practical Section some lyrics are omitted because of copyright restrictions.)

2. SETTLE YOURSELF DOWN

Compose yourself before you start. If you rush into a melody unprepared, then the slightest stumble will be a major blow to your confidence. You will remember the title of the tune and you will, as easily, remember the key in which you play it, but you may not immediately recall the introduction and the starting note, so pause first for the composure that will enable you to recall accurately and with confidence.

3. THE STARTING NOTE

After settling yourself down, you have to develop ways of launching yourself into the body of the tune, and a correct introduction and starting note is all-important. It is inevitable that we are carried through, to some extent, by 'linear' learning – that facet of memory where we remember one piece of information in relation to what comes before it and if we break the 'chain', we're sunk. Make sure the 'chain' gets off to an accurate start! If we are uncertain about the starting or lead-in note, how do we find it with accuracy?....

4. POSITION WITHIN THE SCALE

Already in this chapter we have learned a method of developing our sense of relative pitch. By being aware of our position in the tonic scale and knowing in advance which key we are to play in, then we can work out our starting note with accuracy. So that we can support our memories by the understanding of music and the development of 'ear', let's extend the chart of starting notes you met earlier to provide further examples.

STARTING NOTE IN THE KEY OF C

Tonic C	TIE A YELLOW RIBBON ROUND THE OLD OAK TREE SOMEWHERE OVER THE RAINBOW
D	YOU'RE THE CREAM IN MY COFFEE WHO CAN I TURN TO?
E	ARE YOU LONESOME TONIGHT? GIGI
F	HARVEST MOON YOU'RE THE TOPS
G	HELLO YOUNG LOVERS AROUND THE WORLD
A	GONE WITH THE WIND I DON'T WANT TO WALK WITHOUT YOU
B	DANCING IN THE DARK SERENADE IN BLUE

We can apply our sense of relative pitch at any part of the melody where we may have difficulty in remembering precisely which note is called for. A further tip is to take your practice sessions slowly so that you have time to pause and work out the correct melody rather than to rush in blindly and risk playing the wrong note. But which note is the right one?....

5. THE NOTES OF THE SCALE

We now have the 'sound' of the major scale firmly established in our minds (and in the Theory Revision chapter you will also meet the harmonic minor scale). We know the scale as 1 to 8 or, in arpeggio form, as 1 3 5 8. (Sing the first four words of I COULD HAVE DANCED ALL NIGHT to discover the major arpeggio 1 3 5 8.) From this we appreciate two things:

(a) our basic knowledge of scales tells us which notes we are most likely to meet in any given key,

(b) if we encounter 'accidentals' (notes required which are not catered for by the written key signature), then these 'aliens' stick very prominently in our minds. Imagine in this context melody notes within TAKE THE A TRAIN and DESAFINADO. (The A Train is the train on New York's Underground system that goes to Harlem – now that's something else you'll remember!)

We now have a basic rule of thumb in that we know what notes we expect to meet and if we have any doubts, then we have our 'position within the scale' system to guide our fingers.

6. 'RECOGNITION' NOTES

You will find that the previous two tips will help generally in your music, but if any unusual notes appear within the melody, these will be remembered for their incongruity - if you like, the notes that stick out like a sore thumb! These will almost certainly be accidentals, occuring at a dramatic part of the song and their incongruity and unexpectedness means that they will impress themselves on your memory. Just as in the next chapter you will remember 'the odd man out' in the harmony, so you will remember the melody notes that aren't 'run of the mill'. You can extend this aspect of 'recognition' notes to 'recognition' intervals, where unusually big leaps between melody notes are easily retained in your memory.

7. MELODIES - 'SCALE' OR 'ARPEGGIO' TYPE?

Having now studied the 'sounds' of intervals, how can we categorise our melody for instant recall? When we consider a tune such as DO-RE-MI, we enjoy a lot of repetition in the melody, with each phrase consisting of notes played as if they were sections of a 'scale'. In contrast, perennials such as PRETTY BABY, DAY TRIP TO BANGOR and UP A LAZY RIVER possess much larger intervals between successive notes so that we may loosely call these 'arpeggio' type tunes. Nothing too startling in this, but it does focus our attention on the melody and it is the variety of different approaches that helps instil the melody in our Long Term Memories. Play the musical intervals at the start of the chapter once again to fix this approach in your mind.

8. MELODY AS PART OF CHORD CONSTRUCTION

Just as we looked at melody notes as either falling within the tonic scale or else being memorable as accidentals, so we can anticipate the next chapter on harmony by observing that very often a strong melody note is one of the component notes of the stipulated harmony. The subject of chord construction is covered in the Theory Revision chapter and as we memorise complete tunes we are aware of remembering different aspects at one and the same time - melody, harmony, phrasing, lyrics, etc. and prediction of the melody notes from a sure recall of the harmony is one way of supporting our memory processes.

9. MELODY OVERALL

Never look at melody in isolation. It must be meaningful with regard to the lyrics, dynamics, style and overall 'form'. Consider, too, the introduction and coda so that you interpret the entire piece sympathetically.

General Hints for Memory and Recall

1. Learn to 'hear' accurately. Practise major and minor scales and arpeggios. 'Hearing' correctly means reading the sheet music accurately and listening to your records carefully. It's amazing just how far from the original you sometimes stray when you write your version on to manuscript paper and then compare it with the original!

2. Write the melody out yourself on manuscript paper to focus your attention on the exact notes and the exact timing.

3. Refer constantly to the original to avoid sloppiness and bad habits that will later prove hard to break.

4. Just as with all learning procedures, 'little and often' is far better than con- centrated effort for hours on end. Start with small sections and gradually link them together until the complete melody is at your fingertips.

5. Fingering is a real stumbling block for most people but, with a little foresight the problems can be minimised. You know the notes you are going to play, so lay your hands over the keyboard, encompassing the notes you need, and just see which notes fall comfortably under which fingers. If you are in the key of C, keep that scale of C in your mind where, going up, you crossed your thumb underneath to play the F note, and don't be frightened of crossing fingers over the thumb if that is logical for your requirements. (In the Practical Section we give suggested fingering and in the Theory Revision chapter we cover the subject of fingering in greater depth to help you with your own approach.) Be consistent once you have evaluated the alternatives and this will enable you to play in a smooth and fluid fashion. If it is at all encouraging, there are many professional pianists with fingers missing, and many who perform feats of great dexterity with just two or three fingers! The late genius of the piano, Art Tatum, actually played many cascading right hand runs with just thumb and forefinger, so take heart. If your fingering is logical and efficient and 'works for you' then adopt it, even though it may appear unconventional.

6. Build up right hand technique. Memory is no good if you haven't got the technique to play the tune fluently. Practise the difficult parts and develop your own exercises to develop finger agility. Is there anyone else in the world who 'trills' his 4th and 5th fingers on the steering wheel or plays imaginary runs of thirds on the side of the bath (1 3, 2 4, 3 5, etc.)? Don't skip the awkward bits - the sense of achievement as your playing improves and you find you've mastered them is terrific. A final tip on fingering is to clench your finger and hand muscles and be <u>deliberate</u> in playing each note. Organs equipped with SUSTAIN encourage 'tapping' of the notes, so do be <u>positive</u> as you depress each key.

7. Don't be rushed in your timing. Develop your internal body clock, particularly for the Latin American numbers and tunes with 'gaps'. 'Lean' on the gaps and don't be rushed. Watch the downbeat light to ensure that you give the full value to each note,

and don't insert bars of $3\frac{1}{2}/4$ time! Make sure that you understand the timing in your study examples and if you are unsure, then by all means write over the top of the stave 1 'and' 2 'and' 3 'and' 4 'and' (e.g. for 4/4) to indicate the 4 crotchet beats and also those quavers that may confuse you in between.

8. There are people with total or partial 'photographic' memories. Any additional help you can give yourself, however unmusical, is valid as a means to an end, so if you find yourself able to recall the layout of music 'photographically', then this is yet another boost for melody retention.

9. Review/rehearsal is by far the most important aspect in the chain of memorising. You must, at the end of each practice session, reproduce from memory the section you have just learned. Then maybe after another 15 minutes, do it again. If you do not review the work you have done, then by neglecting this vital link in the chain, you will waste all the effort that has gone before. As we said in Chapter 1, you have a Short Term Memory (STM) and a Long Term Memory (LTM). Short term memories store, on a temporary basis, information recently fed in, such as a casual telephone number which is remembered briefly and then forgotten. However, long term memories store information that you can recall any time you wish (for instance, family telephone numbers), and this information is only stored in the LTM because of practice and repetition - in effect - 'review'. So make sure you don't waste your practice periods by neglecting the review/rehearsal stage that is so necessary to complete the chain of memory. Once you think you have remembered a piece, it should be reviewed again as follows:

Review 1	15 minutes after practice session
Review 2	1 hour after practice session
Review 3	1 day after practice session
Review 4	1 week after practice session

THE IMPORTANCE OF REVIEW

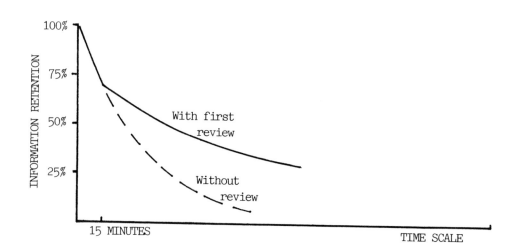

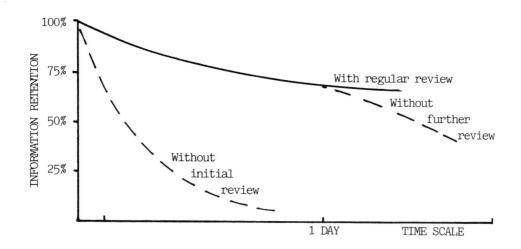

So that you may better relate these specific hints and tips to each Practical Example, we include with each one a MEMORY JOGGERS grid which:

(a) Condenses the list of hints and tips to those with the most frequent application.

(b) Enables you to tick off those which are most appropriate to you and the tune.

MEMORY JOGGERS	
ORGANISATION OF SECTIONS	
REPETITION (sections/lines melody/sequence)	
MATCHING CHORDS TO MELODY NOTES	
"RECOGNITION" NOTES	
"RECOGNITION" CHORDS	
FINGERING	
LYRICS	
"HEARING" THE SOUND	
ASSOCIATION WITH OTHER SONGS	

These, then, are the most important hints and tips. We could provide you with a list of minor ones as long as your arm, but it is the main points that we need to absorb before getting to grips with the practical work. Ideally it would help to read a bit, play a bit and read some more, so that the hints and tips can be seen in their proper perspective as an aid to practical improvement. On now to the chapter on HOW TO REMEMBER HARMONY and, once again, put ticks against the hints that seem appropriate to your own needs.

How to remember harmony

The organist said to the drummer, "It's not fair you know, I have to remember 50 quicksteps, 50 waltzes and 50 disco numbers and you only have to remember 1 quickstep, 1 waltz and 1 disco...." It's not quite as simple as that, but the question does arise, "Now that we've taken the time and trouble to remember several melodies, surely there isn't a further infinite variety of harmonies to remember as well?" Now for the good news - no, there isn't, but we do have to make an effort to organise our harmonies into logical sequences so that these may readily be seen to be self-contained progressions rather than a series of random chords. This is where we come to the chicken and egg situation. Before we can do that, we have to have some knowledge of timing and chord construction which you will find in the THEORY REVISION chapter. Had we put theory at the beginning, most readers would have skipped it, but now that you can start to see its practical importance in conjunction with hints and tips, you will be encouraged to flip back and forth to the theory so that you gain a fuller understanding.

So that we may use our study time to best effect, we have to organise both ourselves and our music. So far, in Chapters 1 and 2, we have looked at ways of organising ourselves and the melody, and now we must study methods of organising the harmony. Below we set out in diagramatic form precisely what is covered in this chapter.

HOW TO ORGANISE THE MUSIC	QUESTIONS & ANSWERS ON REMEMBERING HARMONY	GENERAL HINTS & TIPS ON REMEMBERING HARMONY

1. HOW TO ORGANISE THE MUSIC

So that harmonic patterns and sequences can be easily seen, identified and assimilated let us look at ways of organising the music.

(1) Display the music in 4 bar sections, just as we did for the melody.

(2) Before notating the chords in the modern, accepted fashion, refer to the original sheet music (containing both treble and bass clefs) to ensure that the more modern printed notation is faithful to the original. Our modern notation differs from the original in that we need to specify both the chord and the bass note (where this may differ from the root of the chord stipulated, e.g. Fm means you play an F bass note, but Fm/D requires a D bass.) The theory behind chord notation and construction will be found in the THEORY REVISION chapter.

(3) Once you're sure the chords are correct, simply written, and reflect with accuracy the composer's intention, start to look for chord patterns in relation to phrases and 4 bar sections. To begin with, look at the Practical Section where you will find this chord pattern approach running throughout in tunes of varying complexity, and that will give you the basis to work from when you attempt this approach for yourselves.

(4) Bear in mind that we are not looking at a complete tune, but the sections within it that consist of self-contained sequences that we meet time and time again in our music. Now that you are looking for familiar chord progressions, question whether these progressions conform to any particular harmonic families. You will study later, in the THEORY REVISION chapter, the premise that popular modern chord sequences

can be subdivided into self-contained sequences belonging to one of the following families:

[1] THE CYCLE OF FIFTHS
[2] SIGNIFICANT BASS MOVEMENT
[3] MOVING INTERNAL HARMONY
[4] CHANGE OF TONALITY

If you have trouble remembering the cycle of fifths, don't forget there are mnemonics to help you.

CYCLE OF FIFTHS

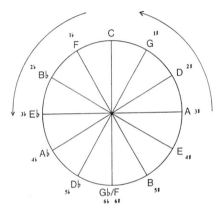

Complete cycle starting on C and moving anti-clockwise: Can Fried Bacon Eggs And Dumplings Give Boys Extra Appetite During Games?

The first clockwise quadrant of the cycle can be remembered by: Alsatian Dogs Growl at Cats.

Just as FACE and Every Good Boy Deserves Favour helped you remember your treble clef, so too you can learn mnemonics to help you remember the cycle of fifths.

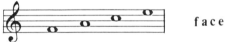

face

egbdf

So although the cycle of fifths is an essential part of our musical education and a good place to start as regards providing a foundation for the 'understanding' aspect of memory development, it is only one family from the four that are later analysed and then introduced progressively in the Practical Section.

(5) The next thing to look for is 'recognition' chords. It is a fact that the more unexpected the chord, the easier it is to retain in your memory. The 'odd man out' syndrome is well documented and it is quite a valid method in 'non-musical' memory development to use something incongruous associated with the fact to be remembered. However, in music, the metronome ticks on remorselessly and we need instantaneous recall in one mental movement to retain our 'flow'. Since we recall the incongruous or unexpected more easily, focus on the 'recognition' chords and use them as land-marks to string the total harmonic sequence together. Imagine yourself in the key of C quite comfortably expecting a progression of A7 D7 G7 C F and, as chord no.2, there appears an alien B7 (e.g. the start of I REMEMBER YOU) – a 'recognition' chord that ultimately you will remember as an extension to the title in this manner: TITLE – I REMEMBER YOU written key of C, starting note B and a second chord of B7. See how we develop this idea in the practical situation where we introduce check charts of MEMORY JOGGERS.

(6) Just for interest, it is intriguing to note that whereas we have adopted a system of chord notation based upon the root notes of the chords, e.g. Dm7 G7 C, we may further condense this by taking away the 'anchor' of C and notating the sequence

as II V I (more easily related to our notation as IIm7 V7 I). You may possibly come across friends who still talk of chord sequences as based upon 1 4 and 5 (C F and G chords in the key of C), so a smattering of this system is handy if you're not to be caught out unawares. However, until you develop absolute familiarity with it, it does presuppose that you first have to remember which degree of the scale the chord is based upon, then relate it to your chosen key - two mental calculations to finish up with one chord and, by and large, our direct system of notation by letters, rather than numbers, is to be preferred. (If you buy a book of French Musettes, the better to accommodate that accordion stop on your organ, you'll find typical harmony instructions written as REm7, SOL7, DO!)

Now that we have started to look at harmonies in more detail, and we find ourselves becoming familiar with the concept that the chord progression is a study subject in its own right, let's introduce a series of general Questions and Answers designed to make our minds more inquisitive whilst at the same time dispelling a few misapprehensions we may have had.

2. QUESTIONS AND ANSWERS ON REMEMBERING HARMONY

(1) What is harmony?

If melody is the skeleton, then harmony is its clothing - items of clothing from a musical wardrobe that fit lots of different melodies, so we learn and remember these small chord progressions that build up to fit many, many melodies.

(2) How do I remember chords and how many have I got to remember?

Everyone likes to make the sort of progress that gives quick results and to that end it is possible to say there is a finite number of chords we are likely to meet, based upon the few familiar keys in which we normally play. However satisfying it may be to remember, say, Am7 Dm7 G7 C & F in their constant application when playing in the key of C, it avoids the issue of 'memory through understanding'. The practical examples gradually introduce you to more and more chords, but if they are not learned through understanding, there is a limit to how many the average student can remember. The only sure way to understand chord construction is to learn your scales and recognise the notes in them and then, (using the advice in the section on Chord Construction in the THEORY REVISION chapter), take whichever degrees of the scale are appropriate and form the chords for yourselves. It's not as difficult as you may think and once you've worked from first principles in the key of C and gained success, you will find that the chords you now understand will become second nature to you. You will get the added benefit that you will understand 'inversions' and, just as your hands will immediately move to the desired chord shape, so you will find that when a particular sequence is required, 'your hands will play it for you'. That's a bonus that comes with practice and familiarity but, for the moment, let's get back to 'memory via understanding'.

(3) How many types of harmonic sequence are there?

Not many, once you recognise the patterns and principles. You will find them in detail at the end of the THEORY REVISION chapter, but basically we can subdivide harmonic progressions into four families, families that conform to:

[1] THE CYCLE OF FIFTHS
[2] SIGNIFICANT BASS MOVEMENT
[3] MOVING INTERNAL HARMONY
[4] CHANGE OF TONALITY

When you've read through the THEORY REVISION chapter and then seen how it works in the practical examples, your memory won't be struggling to remember random information: you will think of it as [1] [2] [3] or [4], each with a meaningful role to play.

(4) How do we remember the cycle of fifths by mnemonics?

Eventually the cycle will become a second language to you but, to start with, think of Alsatian Dogs Growl at Cats and if you are in the key of C you will meet the sequence A7 D7 G7 C time and time again, being chords drawn from the first clockwise segment of the cycle. Admittedly you're not always in C, so a mnemonic to cover all 12 keys is Can Fried Bacon Eggs And Dumplings Give Boys Extra Appetite During Games? We can also further jog our memories by noticing that the word BEAD appears twice in the cycle, once as B♭E♭A♭D♭ and once as BEAD. For an understanding of the construction of the cycle of fifths, please refer to the THEORY REVISION chapter.

(5) What happens if we get lost?

This is more than likely, especially with unfamiliar and unpractised pieces. We remember several things simultaneously - the melody, the lyrics, the harmony, etc. but if the 'thread' disappears, we have to have a method to find it again that doesn't rely on memory alone. If the harmony deserts you, then it is pretty certain you will still remember the melody, so let's develop the idea we first met in the chapter on HOW TO REMEMBER MELODY where we determined which degree of the scale we were on relative to the tonic. You remember that we pinpointed our position by singing up and down in numbers, i.e. we were 3 points adrift from the tonic, for instance. Now, for a change, we have to aurally identify the 'lost' harmony required to support our melody note. Play the melody note, which you know to be accurate and, as you know that the harmony must fall beneath the melody, play downwards and listen to which notes 'fit in' and support the melody. As it is likely that you will be, say, half way through a tune, then it's probably not going to be the tonic note you're looking for as a root to the chord. But, as you play your arpeggio downwards from the melody note, then there will be one chief note that supports the harmony more than the others, and that one will be the root of the chord (often the 'natural' position for your downwards arpeggio to stop), and the significant notes above it will be the notes that are the components of the chord. With this method of ignoring the 'passing' notes and abstracting the 'important' ones, you will jog your memory in identifying the missing chord. Instead of waiting for the 'lost' chord to happen, take a tune for which you know the harmony and play the notes beneath your melody in downward arpeggio fashion to develop this technique. Reading the section on Chord Construction in the THEORY REVISION chapter will also assist your appreciation of this idea. Once you see how your right hand can assist your left hand, you can develop this idea to enable you to play 'block chords' in your right hand.

(6) Is it best to remember chords or bass notes?

NEXT TO MELODY, THE BASS NOTE IS THE MOST IMPORTANT. Since, most often, chords don't specify separate bass notes, you should focus your mind on the bass progression. As you will see from the THEORY REVISION chapter, in families [1] [2] & [3] the bass note is all-important and, what's more, predictable, so your work in remembering is more than halved once you focus on the bass. The bass is easy to remember once we see familiar patterns in it but, all too often, in notating a single stave presentation from the original twin stave music, the bass note is changed for simplicity's sake. This is where your knowledge of chord construction, to be learned in the THEORY REVISION chapter, will stand you in good stead so that you can rewrite the music, faithful to the original, and memorise logical bass patterns.

(7) Do I have to understand chord construction?

Yes, if your music is to have any meaning for you. This doesn't mean to say that you have to have an advanced knowledge - far from it, because most of the time you will be in familiar keys with a limited number of chords. But it does help to know how the chord is built up. From a strictly 'mechanical' viewpoint, even with no 'ear' for music, you will be able to see which chords are compatible with which melody notes and, as a first step in remembering, you could repeat to yourself, "Ah yes, in this tune the F7 chord goes with the C melody note and the E♭ chord fits with the B♭ melody note", etc.

(8) Should I start to remember chord sequences in the way I remember melodies?

Yes, indeed, and it's not as difficult as you may think once you have organised the sequences into sections and stripped away all the vagueness/ambiguity/superfluity on the printed copy that serves only to confuse you. In the Practical Section, we have boiled the chords down to basics so as not to confuse you with details, so take one of the examples that appeals to you and experiment first with memorising the sequence of chords written down, and then play them so that you can appreciate their 'sounds'. Play them with your right hand and bass pedal only, now, and if you are wondering how to start, try putting each chord in its root position. As you start to notice that certain notes are common to successive chords, try making that common note your top note and inverting the chord beneath it to fit in. It doesn't matter how you play them, it's the 'sound of the sequence' that you start to remember, a 'sound' sequence to be considered in isolation and without reference to its role in supporting the melody line, and when we develop this idea, isn't that the basis of what everyone would like to do - improvise?

(9) Do I remember certain chords in certain keys?

Yes, and as we normally play, for the most part, in keys of G, C, F, B♭ and E♭, your work will be made simpler still. Although on paper we can remember small progressions quite easily, when it comes to practice, we may have to stop and think about inversions and often our hands just don't work fast enough. As it is memory in the practical situation that we are developing, it pays to practise the chord shapes and the movement from one chord to another so that you've got the technique to cope with the changes when necessary. You'll need the major and minor chords, of course, and major and minor sevenths so that you can get started, and then as you progress through the practical examples, you will gradually increase your 'repertoire' of chords. If a chord is unusual, by the time you have read the section on Chord Construction, you'll be able to work out its components from first principles so, for heaven's sake, don't think there's any kudos in proudly telling your friends, "I can now remember 45 chords". Remember 20 chords, if you like, but after that the next 200 all come together!

(10) Does it help to recognise chord shapes?

Our purpose is to build up a background for remembering harmony, so it stands to reason that if we've got to stop every other bar to move our fingers into position, the flow is lost. Yes, remember the shapes, they will come naturally after a while, and you'll remember each chord in different inversions too. With each practical example we tabulate suggested inversions so that we promote economy of hand movement coupled with an inversion that 'works' in practice. The configuration of the inversions is all in your mind because if you move to a keyboard with half-size keys, then your mind automatically adjusts everything for you. You will be 'heartened' by the discovery that certain chords appear regularly with different names, so that still further reduces the amount of information you have to programme into your memories. How about the notes C E G A? It looks like a C6 at first sight but, juggled round to A C E G, Am7 rings a bell, with a D pedal it's D11 and with an F pedal it's F9(maj7).

3. GENERAL HINTS AND TIPS ON REMEMBERING HARMONY

These are the sort of pointers you can adapt to any learning and memory situation, so we'll keep it brief and work towards the more important aspect of remembering harmony in conjunction with the melody.

1. Your music is now laid out in 4 bar sections, your chords are basic and logical, so look for the unexpected, the 'recognition' harmony that is unpredictable. Often this comes at a significant part of the melody when there may be a startling choice of notes! Take a good look at that unusual harmony because that is the one that will stick in your mind and the fact that it breaks the music up means that you remember the sequence either side of it more easily. If the harmonic sequence contains such a harmony, we call it the 'recognition' chord.

2. When you are memorising, don't be confused by such details as 6, 9, 11, 13 etc. or such extras as ♯11, -9 and so on, because you'll often find that these are included in the notation to represent the melody note. Keep your chords simple and you will remember them so much more easily - if only because the sequence is already in your memories because you've played it before in other tunes. Consider degrees 1 3 5 7 of the scale as the basic structure of the chord, with degrees 9 11 and 13 the ornamental notes.

3. Chord construction is important because you'll learn to recognise which harmonies fit certain melody notes and which don't, and this will encourage you to listen for the component notes for accuracy and flavour, and to avoid clashes. Use your knowledge of chords to work out the best inversions for sequences which will then 'fall under the fingers' allowing your mind to concentrate on other things.

4. Don't just remember in a vacuum, but write the chord sequences down and then rewrite them from memory. Once you've done that, transfer the chords to the 'sound waves' by playing them from memory.

5. Throughout, when you play and examine chords and sequences so that they may be more easily remembered, always keep the key in which you're playing in mind. It's good to recognise sequences and good to know that often they can pop up in two or three different keys, but another factor that will help you if your memory lets you down is the facet of 'displacement' from the tonic. We've already learned to play the chord in arpeggio form down from the melody in order to identify it so, to that, you can add the concept of 'displacement' from the tonic. Keep the key chord firmly in mind and play your sequences again, just to anchor them down musically to the tonic. You develop two ideas here: (a) the displacement from the tonic which is more obviously heard by listening to the position of the bass note, and (b) the 'feel' of how far into the tune you are. In a sense, there is a time displacement measured in bars, e.g. have we just started the tune, or do we feel that within two or three bars we will return to the tonic? Two ideas for you to ponder on and see if they possess any relevancy to your own studies.

6. Memory in depth doesn't come naturally, we have to prepare ourselves and our music. As regards the aspect of preparing our own approach to memory study, the single most important factor which applies to everyone is the REVIEW. We have both a Short Term Memory and a Long Term Memory and if you don't rehearse/review the material you are trying to learn, then a large proportion of your hard work will be wasted. Just as we reiterate that memory must come through understanding, we continue to emphasise that you must review and rehearse your new material at regular intervals to transfer it from your Short Term Memory to your Long Term Memory.

How to remember melody/harmony together

We have now built up a background of both melody and harmony, and then when we fit them together, we produce the finished article. But to remember two things at once is many times more difficult than remembering each one individually, which is why it is so important to approach both melody and harmony from as many different angles as we can. But what about a technique for putting the two together?

As you work through the Practical Examples, you'll develop your own little tips such as 'the F chord goes with the C melody note' in certain tunes, and you will have the benefit of seeing the chord sequence above the bars so that you may remember, for example, 'two bars of B♭ followed by one of F7'. By all means use this method to assist your memories but treat it as a means to an end. The 'end' product is remembering melody and harmony together to produce the finished article. Three suggested methods are detailed below, each one possessing merit in its different approach, so examine all of them and see which one 'works' for you.

MELODY AND CHORDS TOGETHER - 1ST APPROACH

This method relies on the development of an 'ear' that tells you when a harmony change is due/desirable. In the last chapter, we suggested that you should play the chord sequence on its own, without reference to the melody, to get used to the idea that the harmonic framework was, in its own way, just like a melody line. We learned that we must listen to the 'sounds' of each chord as they progress from one to another and we noticed that the overall sequence could be divided into smaller sequences, each one becoming familiar because (a) it appeared in several different tunes, and (b) it belonged to one of four harmonic families and so it was readily identifiable. (The subject of harmonic families is covered in greater detail in the THEORY REVISION chapter.)

With practice in this method of remembering the chord sequences alone, you are aiming to develop an ability to play the sequence whilst, at the same time, letting the melody line (unplayed) run through your mind. That is the first stage, and then the second stage of this method is to actually put the harmony together with the melody and, in the process of so doing, to develop an 'ear' to predict at which points in the melody line the harmony changes are required. We remember the melody line fairly easily and, on paper, there aren't too many chords in the easier tunes, but the problems arise when we try and fit them together!

It's certainly worth pursuing this line of approach since it's a method that depends on the development of a musical 'ear' rather than a mechanical reproduction and, as such, not only do you achieve memory but, at the same time, you get the additional bonus of developing your musical awareness. By all means start by falling back on the mech- anical aspects, e.g. the C melody note goes with the F7 chord and the B♭ melody note with an E♭ chord in certain tunes, but look further by noting the compatibility between the notes that are components of the chord and the melody note.

To recap briefly, then, remember the chord sequence and then fit it to the melody, developing an 'ear' for the precise position of each harmony change.

MELODY AND CHORDS TOGETHER - 2ND APPROACH

In this method, remember both together all the way, memorising just as much inform-ation as you can comfortably assimilate at any one time. As we actually remember melody fairly easily, so we extend that to encompass its associated harmony and we progress in a complete manner in small, manageable sections. You have to decide for yourselves exactly how much information you can absorb at a time, but it's good advice to set your sights low. You've already seen how sections and phrases are repetitive so decide whether you wish to remember, say, 4 bars or maybe a smaller phrase at any one time.

Study and memorise each small section in isolation and be prepared for the problems that will come when you try to string all the sections together in order to memorise the complete tune. It's often a helpful idea to expand each of your 2 or 4 bar sections to include the starting note of the next phrase/section, so that when the time comes for a complete link-up, everything will flow more readily into place.

Just to recap, break the tune down into small phrases or sections and memorise them individually. Expand each section to include the starting note and chord of the following section and then gradually build up the number of bars that you can remember until you have the complete tune.

MELODY AND CHORDS TOGETHER - 3RD APPROACH

If you are feeling particularly ambitious, it may often help to play the entire tune through several times using the written copy, and to repeat this over the course of several practice sessions. Then, with the familiarity you have developed with the tune, remove the music and attempt to play the complete tune. Invariably you will fail to do so, but this method will pinpoint the specific areas that you need to concentrate on - the weak spots. It's quite a good method of approach as the concept ('shape' or 'form') of the complete piece is in your mind throughout.

On the debit side, you will find the sections you have previously played without thinking or ever considering that you could have trouble with, suddenly, after playing them perfectly dozens of times, become weak spots! It's frustrating but true, so then it's back to the drawing board in order to give them extra attention. The reason for this, of course, is that you failed to understand them musically and once your chain of linear learning faltered, (the chain whereby each part is remembered as following on from the previous part), the thread was broken.

So that you can expose yourself to any potential weak spots, once you feel you have mastered and remembered the tune, play it at half speed. Any slurring or 'fudging' will show up and your fingers won't remember it for you, so if you don't understand what you're doing or your recall is not 100%, then this half-speed exercise will highlight the parts that need extra attention.

MELODY AND BASS TOGETHER AS A BACKGROUND TO UNDERSTANDING

Just as we remember the 'sounds' when we practise a piece of music, so we will remember 'sounds' if we play melody only. It's not what you play, it's what is suggested, and if you're not sure, you have only to insert a slightly wrong chord under your melody and you know immediately that things aren't right. Sometimes it helps us if we play melody and bass line only. There are several good reasons for this:-

(1) It can be habit forming and automatic to play chords continuously - the conscious effort to concentrate on the correct pedal/root notes focuses your attention and makes you select the correct notes.
(2) The playing of chords in set patterns in your left hand means that you often use a sequence where it may not be entirely appropriate. You will certainly fill the sound out for a bar or two, but is it exactly the sequence required?

(3) The aspect of remembering 'sounds' is highlighted by just a bass note and melody. Your mind 'hears' the absent harmony notes, so that when you finally do play them they must be as accurate as you 'heard' them in the first place. (N.B. If you didn't play the piece correctly initially, then you can hardly expect it suddenly to become accurate.)

(4) The two most important parameters in music are the lowest and the highest notes, i.e. bass and melody, and after these are remembered correctly, the harmony notes will slot into place easily.

After this, it is a matter of actually playing the examples yourself and then perhaps, re-reading various sections of the book to see just how relevant each is to your own individual memory processes. You will each have special needs and peculiarities as you will no doubt have realised when you read the first chapter on memory processes and learning strategies, and it is probably comforting to you to realise that you're not alone in all the aspects that give problems in remembering.

Let's finish this chapter now by suggesting a few ideas that you can use. Tick off the ones that appeal to you.

HINTS AND TIPS

1. 'Little and often' is the maxim. Practise and repeat everything a bit every day, never when you're tired, and don't cram too much information in at any one time.

2. Do make sure that you give the 'difficult' bits extra practice and attention because the 'ordinary' bits then become that much easier, and don't forget the essential aspect of repeating and reviewing your freshly learned material.

3. Learn to examine the original with accuracy. Make sure you don't alter the melody to suit what you 'think' you hear, otherwise you'll then find yourself changing the harmony to suit wrong melody notes, which would make it doubly difficult to get back on an even keel.

4. Develop a 'feel' for anticipating significant parts of the tune. Play with expression and get into the 'flavour' of the song.

5. Get confident gradually. Start with an easy piece, knowing that while you are practising and remembering it, you are preparing the groundwork for the more advanced party pieces. The whole essence of memory and recall is time and repetition and review. It just doesn't happen overnight, so start with a simple piece that you would really like to memorise and realise that while you are having success with that, you're gradually getting in your 'time' qualification on a difficult piece.

6. 'A change is as good as a rest', and not only do you benefit from a change but so does your memory. To bombard it with an unremitting diet of the same tune will gradually take away your enthusiasm, so by all means practise 'little and often' but do introduce variety. Your mind still continues to work whilst you are away from the keyboard and often you amaze yourself when, for example, you come back from holiday and find that a lot of information has 'sunk in'. Work hard, then, but don't saturate your memory input with one tune as you'll get there quicker with 'little and often' and 'variety' as your watchwords. And don't forget that what you are remembering in one tune will often be applicable to another.

Theory revision

We call this chapter 'Revision' because it flatters us into believing we already possess the necessary theoretical knowledge to understand the practical work that follows! Even if some of the points are new and fascinating because of a different approach, this chapter overall will consolidate your musical knowledge and give you the confidence to know that you are well equipped to cope with the tunes that follow. Naturally books specifically devoted to Music Theory possess several times the content of this chapter. We are not aiming to study the subject in depth but rather, to revise sufficient theory to enable us to <u>understand</u> the music that we wish to remember.

It is important for us to understand what we are playing before we attempt to memorise it and if we look beyond mere technical dexterity for a goal in our work, let our shining light be, "You must understand and memorise music if you want to make any progress." Memorising makes you get it right because when you attempt to memorise, one of three things happen:

[1] You memorise it correctly and therefore play it correctly.
[2] You memorise it incorrectly and therefore play it incorrectly.
[3] Failing [1] or [2], it means you haven't got it in your memory completely and are
    therefore more likely to play it incorrectly, if at all.

So you have to memorise it properly to get it right, and if you are determined to get it right, that motivates you to memorise it properly.

The key to memory is understanding, organisation and motivation, so having now instilled a high degree of motivation, let's start at the very beginning (DO-RE-MI!) and 'whistle through' enough theory to give us the necessary background with which to tackle the Practical Sections.

We must make three assumptions to begin with:

(1) That readers can play music.
(2) That readers can read music (treble clef and chords).
(3) But that they don't have sufficient knowledge of how music works to enable them
    to remember it.

Below, we show in block diagram form those aspects of music theory that are covered in this chapter.

FINGERING	KEYS AND THEIR RELATIONSHIPS	CHORD CONSTRUCTION	STABLE & UNSTABLE CHORDS	CYCLE OF FIFTHS	HARMONIC FAMILIES

1. FINGERING

Remembering a piece of music is one thing, successful and fluent reproduction is another. So in this first section of THEORY REVISION we approach the tricky, and seemingly taboo, subject of fingering.

There can be no one, correct pattern of fingering for each tune since everyone possesses hands of differing size, shape, dexterity, etc. but we can, nonetheless, offer some guidance as to how we may most logically set about it. With any luck we start with five possibilities, 1 2 3 4 5 where, in popular notation, 1 = thumb, 2 = index finger, 3 = middle finger, 4 = ring finger and 5 = little finger.

The first thing to consider is the comfort of our hands in relation to the notes we wish to play. We look at the range of the phrase we are about to play and see how we can arrange our hands so that the notes will fall naturally under the fingers. This is a start in making our choice of fingers. It may well be that there are more notes than we can encompass in a single span without doubling our fingers over, or thumbs under, at some stage, so let's be specific now with some suggestions.

We have black keys and white keys - long 'uns and short 'uns - and it is a matter of logic that our thumbs cannot extend comfortably to play the shorter black notes so, wherever possible, we need a <u>strong</u> finger for them. We have strong fingers and weak fingers as you will soon discover if you try to over-use your fifth finger, so use 2 3 & 4 unless the black note falls at the top of a phrase, in which case 5 is permissible. When you practise chromatic runs, it should always be your third (middle) finger on the black notes as you alternate between fingers 1 3 and 2 3:

and similarly in descending fashion:

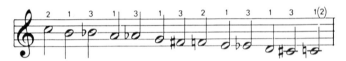

This exercise will promote fluency in your play, strengthen 1 2 & 3, and familiarise you with finger patterns of 1 3 and 2 3.

The fourth finger really comes into its own in scales such as C:

Play both the chromatic and diatonic scales to notice that 2 3 & 4 are strong and flexible whilst 1 & 5 are more limited in what they can do. This introduces you to the concept that in your choice of fingering you should aim at using strong fingers for the important, accented notes.

Now that we have investigated finger patterns of scales, how can we develop this in the practical area where tunes can be either of a 'scale' type (containing melodic phrases with notes in scale type runs) or an 'arpeggio' type (melodies moving in larger than tone intervals). This is where we ally the points made so far: (a) comfort of the hand, (b) emphasis on the stronger digits 2 3 & 4. Imagine chords of C & F both containing upper and lower notes of C, and notice how the 'natural lie' of the hand promotes the use of 4 on the A and 3 on the G. Should you wish to consolidate this fingering, you couldn't do any better than to try a few arpeggios:

which, at the same time, allows your thumb to come into its own by crossing smoothly under your fingers on the white notes. You are now using your whole hand efficiently

31

and when it comes to reproducing a tune from memory, your hands will have developed sufficient technique to avoid obstacles such as 'running out of fingers'!

Now let's tackle the thorny problem of notes that repeat. Imagine a tune such as JINGLE BELLS where the melody note of B (when playing in the key of G) repeats. The straightforward advice is to use just one 'strong' finger that will allow you to complete the phrase comfortably, e.g.

We all take the easy way out at times, by repeating fingers, but should we wish to play JINGLE BELLS at double tempo, then it soon becomes 'jaggedly' apparent that repetition of the same finger is not the solution. Practise the alternative fingering of 3 2 1, 3 2 1:

and before long you will also add repetitions 2 1 2 1 2 1 and 4 3 2 1 4 3 2 1 to your 'fingering repertoire' - especially when you discover how useful they can be when the timing of each note varies.

If we wish to play in a smooth legato fashion, we have to anticipate which fingers to use. Just imagine finishing your phrase on finger 3 and then being faced with a leap to the note lying an octave above! This is where we may swap fingers on the same note, allowing us to anticipate a smooth movement to our next melody note:

We don't really have inflexible rules, only suggestions, and even these are made with a view to you adapting them to your own manual comfort! Let's list a few ideas that may just provide you with a foundation for practice and suggestions to determine your approach.

(1) Fingering patterns will often be suggested. If they appear awkward, don't dismiss them immediately as they obviously work for someone, and what appears illogical initially may be sensible in practice.

(2) Be aware of your fingers' strengths and weaknesses and when you plan your own fingering patterns, relate these to the way your hands naturally cover the keys.

(3) Remembering the music will be doubly difficult if you haven't resolved a logical and consistent finger pattern, since you will inevitably falter in your playing. Plan your fingering, make it comfortable and logical, make it a pattern that 'works for you' and then stick to it.

(4) Don't play the correct fingering in practice and then 'chicken out' in public, but extend your memory of the tune to include the correct fingering. (And don't be tempted to fluff your fingering by gliding your finger off the black notes on to the white ones!)

(5) Use your whole hand, and keep your fingers close to the keys.

(6) Be deliberate in your choice of finger and <u>positive</u> in execution.

(7) There is no better training ground than a book of scales and arpeggios and, surprise, surprise, they really can be fun.

2. KEYS AND THEIR RELATIONSHIPS

As you follow a chord sequence through a tune that appeals to you, you'll notice that certain chords crop up regularly and quite often they appear in tunes that have entirely different key signatures. If you are going to remember music, then you will have to develop an appreciation of what a 'key' is and how the different keys are inter-related. Sometimes the more 'old fashioned' approaches to the subject with super-imposition of 'tetrachords' can be quite daunting with their 'cheese-paring' accuracy, so let's look at this question with a variety of approaches so that you pick up an overall concept that will be meaningful for you. The one thing we must all have in common, however, is the sound of the major scale ringing in our ears, so play the major scale of C:

SCALE OF C MAJOR

and do standarise on this fingering pattern. Now play the same 'sound' in the key of G - start on G, do exactly the same as for our example in C, and notice how you play an F♯ note to retain the same 'sound'. Do the same again starting on F and, lo and behold, the fourth note is a B♭ in order to preserve the 'sound' of the major scale. These, complete with fingering, are illustrated below. (Note that the final note is bracketed in case you wish to play this note with your thumb (1) in readiness for a further octave.)

SCALE OF G MAJOR

SCALE OF F MAJOR

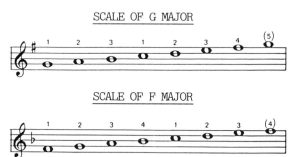

Clearly, if a tune is to flow along smoothly, then it is going to help us to know which sharps and flats we are likely to meet, according to which key we are in. For example, if we are in G, then it's fairly likely that in the course of the melody we will meet an F♯, and if in F, then a B♭ is more or less bound to make an appearance. Not only that, but now that we are starting to think of scales as being useful, we can justify their study still further by thinking of their application to chord construction. The F major chord? Certainly - that's degrees 1 3 & 5 in the F major scale (F A & C) and, should F minor be specified, we merely flatten the third to produce F A♭ & C. G seventh? By now the notes G B D & F loom bold before you, so you think instead of what inversion may be called for. Start to think of keys not only as a succession of notes forming a scale, but an arpeggio, i.e. root, third and fifth (scale degrees 1 3 5), so that you are actually starting to sing out the significant notes themselves rather than including the 'filler' notes in between. This is certainly best for the 'minor' feel as we could get led astray at this stage with differences between harmonic and melodic minor scales. However, once the 'flavour' of the major scale is firmly established in your mind, do consider the alternative flavour of the harmonic minor scale:

SCALE OF A MINOR (The Relative Minor of C Major)

Don't worry too much about its construction but, rather, fix the 'sounds' of the notes in your mind so that when playing in a minor key your ears will tell you which notes are likely to be encountered. More important at this stage is to remember the sound of the minor arpeggio:

ARPEGGIO OF C MINOR (The Relative Minor of E♭ Major)

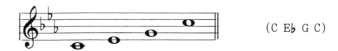

(C E♭ G C)

and to note that, from a practical point of view, C Minor is written with a key signature of E♭, A Minor with the key signature of C, etc., because C Minor is the relative minor of the key of E♭ and A Minor is the relative minor of the key of C.

Why are tunes played in different keys and what determines their choice?

(1) Vocal

(a) Voice range of singers often determines key. In general terms, a tune should be pitched to build the climax to notes not exceeding C or D (the high notes normally come at the climax of the tune). Exceptions would be songs by Tom Jones, Neil Sedaka, etc., where general playing is in a key lower than that written.

(b) Ballads tend to be played in 'flat' keys, e.g. A♭, E♭, B♭, F etc. for reasons of temperament mentioned later.

(c) Bright'n'breezy songs tend to be played in 'sharp' keys for the same reason.

(d) These last two points combine to make us aware that different keys have 'flavours' – E♭ is mellow whereas a seemingly insignificant shift of a semitone produces 'bright', 'hard' keys of D or E. Again investigate 'temperament' and even think about relating colours to keys to give a subjective impression of 'flavour'.

(e) Some keys are 'obligatory', e.g. THE NATIONAL ANTHEM is always played in G, TEA FOR TWO is always played in A♭ and BODY AND SOUL should always be played in D♭!

(2) Instrumental

Which instrument is the tune designed for?

(a) Keyboard players don't mind which key they're in. Investigate Bach's WELL TEMPERED CLAVIER which runs through every key and exhibits the character of each.

(b) Guitars like the key of E because of the way they are tuned. Hence much guitar-based music is written in E and A.

(c) Saxophones like A♭, E♭, B♭ and F etc. since when the concert key is E♭, an alto saxophone plays in his key of C – a lot more comfortable for sight reading than F♯!

(d) Similarly clarinets and trumpets prefer keys such as E♭, B♭, F and C.

If we work on the principle that we change the character and 'flavour' of a song with a change of key, then it follows that if we all have a common perception with regard to the flavour/interpretation of a song, then there could and should be one standard key in which it should be played.

One surprising point is that the choice of this one particular key does not apply to organs, though it DOES apply to pianos. This is because each interval on an organ is precisely the same - the subdivision of the octave being directly related to the 12th root of 2 - which means that each semitone interval is precisely the same as its neighbour. This restriction does not apply to a piano, and for further information on this subject you are referred to the section on TEMPERAMENT and THE ASSOCIATION OF KEYS WITH COLOUR in The Oxford Companion to Music by Dr. Percy Scholes. However, although the organ precludes natural reactions to 'brightness' and 'dullness' of certain keys, we still have conventions and singers' ranges to guide our choice of key.

Now that we've practised a few scales and got major and minor flavours in our minds, it's time to relate this information to the subject of chord construction so that you have the solid appreciation of chord theory that is so necessary if you are to memorise via understanding.

3. CHORD CONSTRUCTION

Once the right hand is taken care of, the next important aspect is that of the chords to be played with the left hand. Although you can achieve satisfying results by remembering some familiar, well-used chords that may be adequate for a restricted repertoire, it is at this point that we must question these chords because we must now approach harmony from the standpoint of notes, rather than one familiar inversion and a chord shape that falls under the fingers. Ask a friend to play Am7, for example, and his left hand moves like an eagle's talons, descends to the keyboard, hovers, and after rejecting adjacent familiar chords, finally settles in triumph! We've got to be precise in our identification of the exact notes required from our knowledge of the construction of the chord, so that we will be able to use any inversion that may be appropriate for our needs. Don't forget, you have only to learn the principles of chord construction once, and they apply to any key in which you play, not that you will want to set the world on fire in six sharps, but it will mean that you'll become more fluent in the more regular keys and, if it's further encouragement you want, you'll find that memory really will be helped through an understanding of chord construction.

Let's now look at chord construction and notation. Since all the necessary information may be presented to you in just treble clef for the melody and a chord symbol for the harmony and the bass line, we've got to get to grips with the modern form of notation that represents the composer's intentions.

If we want a simple C chord, we take notes 1 3 & 5 from the C scale, C E & G. If we want a C7 chord we add the flattened (minor) seventh note of the C scale, Bb, so C7 is C E G Bb. If we want Cmaj7 we add the major seventh note of the scale, B, to the basic C chord, so Cmaj7 is C E G B. If we want a basic C chord, but played with an E pedal, then we call it C/E.

Chords are mainly made up of successions of thirds, and these musical intervals may be either major or minor thirds, built up in varying combinations. It may clarify a point here for you to sing the major arpeggio (triad) of the scale of C, degrees 1 3 & 5 corresponding to the notes C E & G. The interval C to E is a major third (four semitone intervals), and that of E to G is a minor third (three semitone intervals), so it's comforting to realise that major and minor thirds exist happily side by side and it's just a way of analysing what occurs naturally in our music. When we flatten the third degree of the scale to get Cm, C Eb G, then the first interval becomes a minor third and the second, a major third (a reversal of C major, C E G).

Off we go now up two octaves of the scale of C major as follows:

1	3	5	maj7	9	11	13						
C	D	E	F	G	A	B	C	D	E	F	G	A	B	C

Let us now clarify that possibly misleading point of notation: why, if we call a chord C7, does it contain a B♭ as its seventh and not the B that appears as the seventh degree in the major scale? The most straightforward explanation is that C7 is the dominant seventh of the scale of F, the note of C being the fifth, or dominant, note in the F scale. As such, we may consider a C7 chord as being derived from the F scale and the notes therein. We construct a C7 chord with degrees 1 3 5 & 7 based on a C root, and those component notes 1 3 5 & 7 will be notes that fall naturally within the F scale, i.e. C E G B♭.

We may now distinguish comfortably between C7 and Cm7 (notes of C E G B♭ and C E♭ G B♭ respectively) and Cmaj7 where the notation specifies the inclusion of the major seventh note, B natural.

Observe also that the B♭ note in the dominant seventh chord, C7, is the 'unstable' component that urges the chord to resolve to the next point around the cycle of fifths, moving in an anti-clockwise direction.

As we have already stated, consider degrees 1 3 & 5 of a scale as constituting the 'body' of a chord whilst degrees in excess of 7, i.e. 9 11 13, add 'flavour' and are considered ornamental notes.

Now it's all plain sailing and whatever notes we wish the musician to play, can be specified numerically with the addition of sharp, flat and natural signs to indicate accidentals (that is, notes not appearing in the major scale). The only rule is that if we specify an odd number greater than 7, e.g. a ninth or eleventh, then we assume the inclusion of the 7th as a contribution to the bulk (or body) of the chord and to keep the 'unstable' element included. Here are a few examples:

C7	=	C	E	G	B♭	
Cmin7	=	C	E♭	G	B♭	
C9	=	(C)	E	G	B♭	D
Cmin9	=	(C)	E♭	G	B♭	D

This is quite straightforward and once the idea of building basic chords in thirds is appreciated, then you've mastered chord construction. The question now is, "Why do we always seem to include root, third and fifth, and when do we run out of fingers?" Well, a chord has to have some 'body' to it and it is very helpful to start by putting in as much of this harmonic content as we can. We may include root, third and fifth as normally these provide a fullness to the chord without clashing (or causing dissonance) with the intended sound. It is only when you understand these principles that you can be selective about which components to omit. As the bass note is normally an octave or more below the register in which we play our harmony chord, then we would very often omit the root from our chord, which is why we've put brackets around the C's in the table above. The next one to go as it's often only a 'filler' is the fifth, and by this process a C9, for example, could become E B♭ D – a nice 'open' harmony without the clutter of the C and G.

Keeping everything to basics, the golden rules are just four – if it's major, play major, minor play minor, if the degree of the chord exceeds 7, e.g. a thirteenth, you'll always get away with playing a seventh and, lastly, if you see signs of 6, ♯11, 13 etc., nine times out of ten these represent the melody note, so you may, if you wish, ignore these signs and keep the accompaniment simple and uncluttered by playing the basic chord.

Let's take a 'breather' here, rather than get bogged down in the theory of 'dis-integrated' ninths and 'demolished' elevenths, by taking as an example a simple Am7. You now have the advantage over your colleagues (we've got to nurture that competitive instinct in you!) by knowing how to construct the chord from first principles. Counting up from the root it's 1 3 5 & 7. 1 is our root note A, 3 is the minor third C (minor, because it was specified in the notation Am7), 5 is E which is the fifth note of the scale of A, and 7 is the unstable component, the flattened seventh, G – A C E G, to be played in whatever inversion is called for, and as there are four notes, it stands to reason that there will be four inversions: A C E G, C E G A, E G A C, G A C E. Experiment yourself with these to get those sluggish left hand fingers responding to the messages from your brain, and although you may tend to favour the last inversion G A C E because it falls in a nice area of the keyboard (neither too 'muddy' nor too 'shrill', with 8' stops on the registration), it may well be that the preceding or following harmonies demand a different inversion for economy of left hand movement, (i.e. keep your left hand fairly still rather than leaping all over the keyboard in order to play the only inversion you know!).

As we encounter chords of special significance in the examples later in the book, we'll look at them individually, but for now we'll leave the revision on chord con-struction and touch on some more aspects that may help your understanding of more modern approaches to music study.

4. STABLE AND UNSTABLE CHORDS

A little earlier we referred to the subject of an 'unstable' component within a chord, so let's now extend our basic knowledge of chord construction to encompass the aspect of stable and unstable chords. You will have noticed in your music how the chords you meet tend to be a mixture of majors, minors, sevenths, etc. and you have probably always accepted this without question. Let's first look at the stable chord, often just a major triad (C E G in the key of C) that sits quite happily where it is with no desire to move on unless the melody progresses and requires a different harmony to support it. Once that happens, and we get into the tune, we start to meet unstable chords – chords that are nearly always based on 'sevenths', that can be used to support the melody for a short while and which then 'resolve' to more unstable chords until the melody line finishes and we're back to our tonic chord again. Once we're home and dry again in our 'key chord', then we're stable. The melody has completed its sequence and has been supported by a succession of 'transient' chords, each resolving to the next in the progression until ultimately we return home to the key chord. Throughout the sequence we normally retain the 'tonality' of the key chord in our minds so that once the unstable chords have progressed through their sequence, we know instinctively when we're back home.

The degree of stability or instability may be promoted by extra notes in the con-struction of the chord. For stable chords, you will most frequently see an added sixth, e.g. C6 is C E G A and, to a lesser extent, the major seventh and ninth notes (notes of B and D in the scale of C). Degrees of instability may be promoted by the inclusion of the 'seventh' (Bb in the scale of C), the augmented fifth (G♯) and, together with the seventh (Bb), notes such as the 9th, flattened 9th, 11th and 13th (D, Db, F & A) which are included to impart different 'flavours'. Play a few to get the flavour in your minds, but, more importantly, observe how we arrive at the construction of these chords so that you will be able to pick out these 'flavours' in any key.

C	=	C	E	G		C7	=	C	E	G	B♭
Cm	=	C	E♭	G		Cm7	=	C	E♭	G	B♭
C6	=	C	E	G	A	C+	=	C	E	G♯	
Cmaj7	=	C	E	G	B	C9	=	(C)	E	G	B♭	D
C6/9	=	(C)	E	G	A	D					

A further, essential, flavour to retain in your mind is that of the diminished seventh chord - written as C° or Cdim - and constructed of a series of minor third intervals, C E♭ G♭ A, each minor third interval containing three semitones. Diminished chords don't possess a tonality of their own and are useful devices to introduce harmonic variety, and in their application as 'bridging' chords to link up two more 'regular' chords. They are rarely used in succession (unless you wish to heighten a sense of drama, e.g. accompaniment to silent movies!), and once you have learned C° C♯° and D° then they merely repeat, possibly in different inversions, for the remaining root notes, i.e. C° = E♭° = G♭° = A° and so on.

These basic chord 'flavours' are enough for our purposes in developing the memory aspect of playing and, if you are fascinated by the more advanced notations, then please obtain specialist books on the subject.

Now it's time for a diagram so that the relationship of one key to another is immediately apparent and, furthermore, their relative positions in the diagram have a very important practical application. The cycle of fifths, as a representation of the relationship of keys, has been with us for over fifty years and really is an essential part of our musical education.

5. THE CYCLE OF FIFTHS

(1) Diagram of the cycle of fifths showing key signatures and relative minor keys

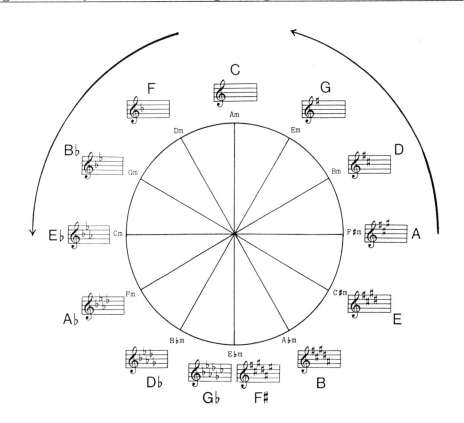

Sit at your keyboard and place a finger on middle C. Counting C as 1, and moving up 5 notes in the scale of C, you come to G (the key with one sharp). Then counting G as 1, and moving 5 notes up in the scale of G, you come to D (the key with 2 sharps). After repeating this operation 12 times (falling back on the keyboard as necessary to avoid running out of notes), you return to C. This is a clockwise movement around the cycle of fifths, in fifth intervals. Repeating the operation, but this time going anti-clockwise around the cycle of fifths, place a finger on top C. Counting C as 1, and moving 5 notes down the scale of C, you come to F (the key with 1 flat). Then counting F as 1, and moving 5 notes down the scale of F, you come to Bb (the key with 2 flats). Again, if you repeat this operation 12 times, you come back to C. This is an anti-clockwise movement around the cycle of fifths, again in fifth intervals.

(2) Cycle of fifths rules

[1] If a tune conforms to the principles of the cycle of fifths, you may move, at the commencement of a chord sequence, away from the tonic in a clockwise direction, as many degrees as the harmony requires and then return to the tonic in an anti-clockwise movement via a series of sevenths (unstable chords), one degree at a time, e.g. C, A7, D7, G7, C.

[2] At any stage of a tune or chord progression, you may encounter small, self-contained sequences conforming to the movement predicted by the cycle of fifths.

[3] If you progress anti-clockwise from the key chord, then it is normally through one degree only, e.g. C7 to F.

[4] The majority of chords you will encounter will be based on root notes which fall in the first quarter of the cycle clockwise from the key chord plus the root note which lies one degree anti-clockwise (and, just occasionally, the one that lies two degrees anti-clockwise) from the key chord, e.g. the chords you would be most likely to encounter in the key of C would be based on forms of A7 D7 G7 C & F.

[5] A dominant seventh chord will nearly always move to the next degree anti-clockwise, e.g. C7 to F, F7 to Bb, etc.

[6] If you wish to find a substitute/alternative chord, it may fall on the opposite side of the cycle 'across the spokes', e.g. Dm7 G7 C could be substituted by Dm7 Db7 C where Db is diametrically opposite G and may be used as an alternative. Note how this use of alternative chords can give rise to chromatic bass movement, e.g. D Db C.

(3) Tips on the use of the cycle of fifths

[1] The sequence of keys around the cycle can be remembered by the mnemonic Can Fried Bacon Eggs And Dumplings Give Boys Extra Appetite During Games? (i.e. C F Bb Eb Ab Db Gb B E A D G).

[2] The quadrant of the cycle clockwise from C can be remembered as Alsatian Dogs Growl at Cats. It is also useful to note that the word BEAD appears twice around the cycle as Bb-Eb-Ab-Db and also as B-E-A-D.

[3] When a change of tonality occurs between sections of a song, in many cases the new key lies either a major or minor third away, and cycle rules may then be applied to the new tonality.

[4] Not all harmonic sequences can be predicted by the cycle, but it is a starting point and a good visual aid that will promote familiarity with all keys, and its rules do apply to the majority of tunes, nearly always in part and sometimes completely.

To bring this explanation into the realms of 'sound', a page or two ago we invited you to play the major scale of C to introduce and establish the sounds of each note relative to one another. Now count 5 notes up the scale of C to reach G and play the major scale of G. Notice how one sharp is present within this new scale - a key signature containing one sharp. When you extend this by counting up five degrees in the scale of G, you reach D, and when you play the major scale of D you notice how this becomes the key signature containing two sharps, and so we go on progressing either in a sharp or flat direction. We've now established an interrelationship based on the diagram and our 'sounds' above. The relevance of all this we start to see in our music when we realise that if, for example, we are in the key of C we encounter, most frequently, these interrelated <u>chords</u> in the first clockwise segment of the cycle of fifths. Just as we saw previously, when in the key of G we would expect to meet the melody note of F♯, now we see that if in the key of G we would expect to meet harmony <u>chords</u> based upon root notes of D A & E. When we develop this aid to memory, these are the pointers that are going to enable us to memorise more quickly and with more accuracy. We have already stated that in whichever key we find ourselves, we will normally have the key chord as a 'stable' chord with the remaining chords unstable, so as to lead us back to our stable key chord. With reference to the cycle of fifths, we can now predict (or anticipate) which will be the most likely chords that we will meet. At this stage we ought to make it clear that this isn't by any means a complete guide to D.I.Y. composition and interpretation, but it does give us a starting point for harmonic recognition in tunes either partially or wholly conforming to the rules of the cycle of fifths. Rules for the use of the cycle in a chord progression application have already been tabulated, but our main purpose at this stage is to gain a pictorial representation (via the cycle) of all keys in a logical format, so that adjacent keys can be seen to be relative. We first met the concept of 'keys' back in the chapter on HOW TO REMEMBER MELODY. So important is an awareness of key - often a subject that is overlooked completely - that the explanation stands repetition as a foundation for the theory that is to follow.

What is a key? A key, and the melodies and harmonies performed in that key, are all bound together in a common relationship to a single note, the key note or tonic. Consider the key note to be the stable foundation note and you will start to appreciate that at any part of the tune your melody and harmony are not to be considered in isolation, but in relation to the stable tonic key note. Keys may change in pitch, and the scales based upon key notes may differ (major, minor, etc.) but once the initial 'home' key is established, all subsequent melodies and harmonies possess an identity relative to the key/tonic note.

6. HARMONIC FAMILIES

So far we have examined many aspects of music in a fashion which invites the reader to determine which approach works best for himself. Style, unpredictability, originality; there are so many facets that go towards the fascination of music that there can be no one thread of tuition that is progressive and complete at one and the same time. Everyone has different requirements so that it is difficult to say which aspects should be covered first and which ones should be ignored. However, since our brief is the development of memory in its application to popular music, we must leave pure theory behind for the moment in an attempt to clarify and organise our music into categories that may be most easily understood. For this reason, so that our recall of the tunes we will memorise later may be via understanding, we must look at aspects of the composition of harmonic sequences.

It would seem helpful to organise our approach to composition by analysing our music in relation to four categories. In general, we appreciate music because of the unique thread that runs throughout, a thread that for one reason or another binds it together to make that tune like no other. A series of random chords holds no fascination for us as it is threadless, so with that in mind, what is it that may appeal to us in our favourite tunes? Is it the melody? And, if so, isn't it just as likely to be the attraction of the chord sequence that supports the melody? Is it a dramatic change of harmony that is majestic in its effect or could it be a subtle change of harmony supporting a simple, repetitive melody line? Let's start to focus our minds by organising the harmonic aspect of the tune into four categories (or families), bearing in mind that all four could be present within one tune or just one alone. (We don't mention melody at this stage, since it is assumed that if you like the tune in the first place, whether you sing the lyrics, hum or even whistle it, the melody by one sense or another is firmly established in your mind.) The four harmonic families we are going to examine are:

[1] THE CYCLE OF FIFTHS
[2] SIGNIFICANT BASS MOVEMENT
[3] MOVING INTERNAL HARMONY
[4] CHANGE OF TONALITY

When you come to the practical examples, you will find a grid included in our disucssion of the harmonic principles involved, so that you will have an immediate visual reference of the harmonic structure of the composition.

HARMONIC PRINCIPLES ILLUSTRATED			
CYCLE OF FIFTHS	SIGNIFICANT BASS MOVEMENT	MOVING INTERNAL HARMONY	CHANGE OF TONALITY

[1] THE CYCLE OF FIFTHS

This we have already met, but now that your attention has been drawn to it, you will observe it in virtually every tune you play. Even if its principles/rules only apply for a few bars or so, this will help your analysis and understanding of the tune and will therefore assist your memory. The beauty of the situation is that once you have started to recognise the cycle's application, you'll meet it time and time again - hard work for the mind in the first place, but dividends repaid a thousandfold later.

[2] SIGNIFICANT BASS MOVEMENT

Of course, the bass line moves in cycle sequences, but it is when it moves in small, regular intervals that it becomes significant and interesting. You must always think first of the two outside parameters in your music: the melody note in the treble, and the bass note at the bottom, supporting the harmony. When you appreciate that the 'flavour' of the harmony is dependent for the most part on the bass note, you can see how important it is and why it deserves special mention. You start to see the interrelationship of our studies so far when you realise that to interpret the significance of any bass movement we must necessarily have a working knowledge of chord construction which, in turn, depends upon a knowledge of scales. All this becomes clearer in the practical applications, but imagine for now a little trip around the cycle from C to F via C7, i.e. C C7 F. When we examine the construction of each chord we get:

```
C    = C   E   G
C7   = C   E   G   Bb
F    = F   A   C
```

Just imagine we wish to promote 'tension' and 'urgency' in the flavour of the tune, then a favourite trick is to make the bass line ascend and we can justify this by using an appropriate note from the C7 chord notated as follows: C C7/E F

```
C   =      C   E   G
C7  = C    E   G   Bb
F   =      F   A   C
           |
```

ASCENDING BASS LINE

The opposite may be required for a 'mellow' flavoured descending bass line, e.g. C C7/Bb F/A

```
C                      C   E   G
C7      C   E   G      Bb
F               F      A   C
                       |
```

DESCENDING BASS LINE

In these examples it helps to keep our principles of the cycle of fifths in mind, but what of Bach's AIR ON THE G STRING where the bass movement is the significant part for our memory to focus upon? It is unlikely that the T.V. adverts for cigars would have used this theme had it had a disturbing, ascending bass line! If cigars help you to remember the flavour of this tune by means of the television advertisement association, then it may be unmusical but it's certainly valid from a memory point of view.

[3] MOVING INTERNAL HARMONY

In this third harmonic family, it is the internal harmony that moves whilst the bass line remains static. This is often referred to in popular music as a 'pedal' bass which means that the bass note is static and the harmony above it moves in a succession of chords which may or may not be related to the bass note. You will meet the moving internal harmony with static bass in two main applications:

(1) In tunes such as THE DAM BUSTERS MARCH (Practical Example 27) where, in the introduction sequence, a sense of drama is built by superimposing ascending harmonies over a 'pedal' bass note, and

(2) As the foundation for 'filler' sequences, i.e. moving internal harmonies that provide interest without disturbing the overall tonality, e.g. GENTLE ON MY MIND and EL CUMBANCHERO (Practical Examples 10 and 20).

[4] CHANGE OF TONALITY

In pieces of music that are considered 'evergreens' today, and that usually means composed twenty or more years ago, the normal format was AABA. Theme A was repeated, followed by Miidle Eight B before returning to the original theme once again to conclude the tune. In this type of layout it was more or less certain that the Middle Eight (Section B) would change in tonality (key) to provide variety. Notice, however, that the key signature of the piece did not normally change in this Section (to avoid introducing confusion), but your ears most definitely told you that a different tonality from the original was present. In Example 18, I COULD HAVE DANCED ALL NIGHT, you will observe two pronounced changes of tonality in Section B, tonalities of E & G before reverting to the written key of C for final Section A.

For our study purposes, we may also consider as a change of tonality sections of the same tune which differ in flavour, one being major and one minor (e.g. Y VIVA ESPANA). Often there will be a transient change of tonality within a tune that quickly resolves back again and we can also, for convenience, consider this temporary change of 'flavour' as a change of tonality (e.g. bars 1 & 2 of GOLDFINGER $\boxed{C\,|\,A\flat}$ and bars 1 & 2 of I REMEMBER YOU $\boxed{C\,|\,B7}$

This concludes the THEORY REVISION as general background with regard to theoretical knowledge and its application. As we progress through the three sections of practical work, BASIC, INTERMEDIATE and ADVANCED, when a specific point of interest crops up that hasn't been covered, then we'll refer to it in detail. Music theory is a fascinating study, but we must keep our feet on the ground and align it to its purpose in this book, that of aiding our memories. For that reason it is important for us to feel that theory is a tool for us to use in our studies, rather than be overwhelmed by the thought that it is infinitely complex and beyond our comprehension. Perhaps we should paraphrase this thought in the form of 'Familiarity breeds not contempt, but attempt'! If you need any further encouragement to immerse yourself in your music in a confident, sure-footed way, then always remember that music is there for your enjoyment and it matters not which level of ability you're at, everyone can derive the same degree of pleasure.

Let's move on now to our first practical section - BASIC - where you are invited to pick out a tune that is familiar to you. This will give you a head-start in the sense that you are already half way towards knowing the tune and you will have the motivation to succeed.

BASIC SECTION

EXAMPLE	JINGLES	SONGS FOR SPECIAL OCCASIONS	EVERGREENS/ STANDARDS	PRACTICE OR PARTY PIECES
1	NON-MUSICIAN'S JINGLE			
2	CHOPSTICKS			
3		HAPPY BIRTHDAY TO YOU		
4		JINGLE BELLS		
5		SHOW ME THE WAY TO GO HOME		
6		AULD LANG SYNE		
7		ANNIVERSARY WALTZ		
8			SPANISH EYES	
9			I LOVE YOU BECAUSE	
10			GENTLE ON MY MIND	
11			KISS ME, HONEY HONEY	

1. The Non-Musician's Jingle

SUGGESTED CHORD INVERSIONS							
F	F A C	C	G C E	G	G B D	Am	A C E

This is an interesting jingle to play and remember once we understand how it evolved. If you take the major triad of C (C E G) which, in 'unmusical' terms is C, miss one, play one, miss one, play one (all on the white notes), and then move your left hand two white notes down to start on an A and repeat the process, then again two down to F and finally one up to G, you get the chord sequence C Am F G. Nothing too startling musically, but nonetheless interesting and 'mechanically' very easy to remember.

STRUCTURE				
WRITTEN KEY	STARTING/LEAD-IN		TEMPO/RHYTHM	ORGANISATION OF SECTIONS
	NOTE	CHORD		
C	C	C	6/8 MARCH ♩. 112	-

When we start to remember music, we develop a memory of 'associations' Mention GOD SAVE THE QUEEN to any musician and he'll tell you to play it in G. In this way we may extend our memory of the title to include KEY, STARTING NOTE, TEMPO and the ORGANISATION of the piece (i.e. Verse, Chorus, Verse or 'A' 'A' 'B' 'A' etc.) We play this jingle in the key of C, we start on a C note and a C chord, the tempo has the triplet feel of a 6/8 march and 'organisation' doesn't really come into this one as we are only playing a repetitive 4 bar pattern.

HARMONIC PRINCIPLES ILLUSTRATED			
CYCLE OF FIFTHS	SIGNIFICANT BASS MOVEMENT	MOVING INTERNAL HARMONY	CHANGE OF TONALITY
			✓

As this is our first exercise, we will probably be looking for all the 'non-musical' help we can get — the sort described in the first paragraph! However, the purpose of each graded example is to improve our memories via understanding, so we have to abstract as much information from each example as possible. As you play this 'self-contained' 4 bar sequence you will notice that it could well pass for an introduction sequence, and in fact it could also be the basis for a 'vamp' in C. We have ticked the box in the above grid for a change of tonality as this 'one-off' sequence is simply a succession of 'stable' chords (i.e. not sevenths) that, together, form a pleasing progression. Start thinking of our harmonic movements stretching out from C on a piece of elastic — we can move away up to the limit of the 'stretch', but inevitably we are pulled back home at the end of each sequence. In this case the elastic pulls three ways: (1) first away from C to its relative minor, C to Am, and then (2) to the point one degree anti-clockwise on the cycle of fifths (F), and (3) finally to the point one degree clockwise on the cycle of fifths (G). This means that if you wish to consider playing this jingle in any other key, you have only to refer to the cycle of fifths in your mind to predict the chords you will encounter. Let's take the key of E♭ as an example:

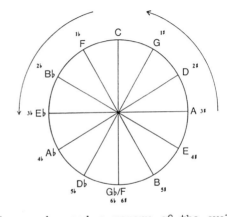

    (a) E♭ to its relative minor - Cm
    (b) E♭ to one point anti-clockwise - A♭
    (c) E♭ to one point clockwise - B♭

Thus we arrive at E♭ Cm A♭ B♭ for our sequence. We cannot predict this pattern mechanically since these chords all contain 'black' notes and the fingering pattern would therefore change. So this is an instance where successful memorising involves <u>understanding</u> the cycle. You need not be musically gifted to transpose a sequence, but you do need a memory of the cycle layout, and this exercise will build confidence for later examples where a more 'musical' understanding of principles will assist our memory processes.

MEMORY JOGGERS	
ORGANISATION OF SECTIONS	
REPETITION (sections/lines melody/sequence)	√
MATCHING CHORDS TO MELODY NOTES	√
"RECOGNITION" NOTES	
"RECOGNITION" CHORDS	
FINGERING	√
LYRICS	
"HEARING" THE SOUND	√
ASSOCIATION WITH OTHER SONGS	

As you will see from the accompanying grid, we've ticked the boxes that relate to this, our first example. The phrases are repetitive, the fingering is repetitive and the aspect of relating melody notes to the chord symbol is self-evident since we are, in fact, playing the arpeggio of each chord as our melody line. The melody/arpeggios, when we stop to <u>listen</u> to them carefully, register in our <u>store</u> of sounds, so that our memories gradually start to build a repertoire of chord sounds (i.e. major, minor, sevenths, etc.) plus an appreciation of these chord sounds grouped together in progressions. This idea will later enable us to remember tunes so much more easily as, if a section of one tune is similar to a section in another, we have only to remember it once, and thereafter we recall by a process of cross-reference. As you will later see, melodies are always different, but the same harmonic sequences crop up everywhere.

Let's now put into practice that aspect, from the chapter on HOW TO REMEMBER MELODY, of 'hearing' which note of the scale we start on so that we can abstract still more from this example to teach ourselves a 'procedure' for memorising and recall. When you wish to play any piece from memory, it is important to settle yourself so that you may start accurately, using the correct notes. You don't need to play any notes at this stage. Just start to sing the melody to yourself in your mind, and ask yourself what degree of the scale you start on. (See page 12 in HOW TO REMEMBER MELODY.) Not the third, fourth, fifth, etc. but the tonic so, remembering that the piece is in the key of C, you know you will start on a C note. Similarly you will develop the feel that in this example you play the tonic chord of C to accompany your first melody notes. Although the starting note could and should be remembered along with the title, this method of working out the starting note for ourselves is useful to fall back on if our memories falter. When you take time to 'settle' youself before starting, you'll find that everything that follows will flow more easily.

2. Chopsticks

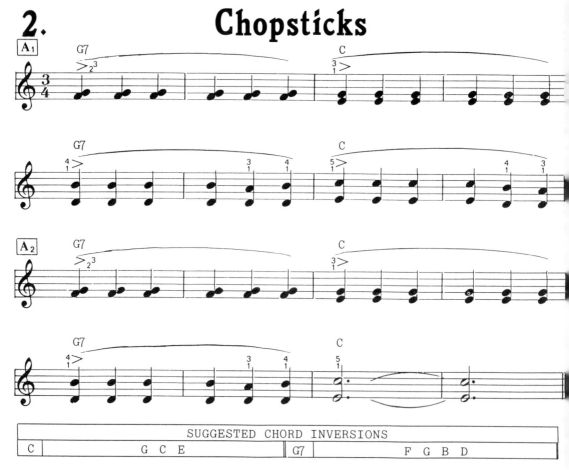

SUGGESTED CHORD INVERSIONS		
C	G C E	
	G7	F G B D

Not everyone's cup of China tea, but still a good example for many reasons. Even though it is simple and unambiguous, it's well nigh certain that you will make mistakes when you turn the page and attempt it from memory – and it's from these mistakes that you will learn not only more about the tune, but also more about yourself.

STRUCTURE				
WRITTEN KEY	STARTING NOTE	LEAD-IN CHORD	TEMPO/RHYTHM	ORGANISATION OF SECTIONS
C	G	G7	FAST 3/4 ♩ = 240	A₁ A₂

Jingles are intriguing, musically, since often they are played all on the white notes or all on the black notes. Luckily for us, CHOPSTICKS is all on the whites and, as such is in the key of C. It is in fast 3/4 time (♩ = 240) as opposed to a typical ballroom waltz of around ♩ = 96, and the organisation is such that you will notice that Section A₂ more or less repeats section A₁ so that once you've mastered the first 6 bars of A₁ you'll find them repeated in Section A₂. The accents fall at the start of each 2 bar phrase and the phrasing lines ensure that each sub-division of 2 bars is separate. There are only two chords to remember, G7 and C, and these alternate – the interesting point being that we start on G7 instead of the tonic.

Let's pause for a while to discuss that aspect of assisting our memories by 'hearing' the starting note and starting chord. As we saw back in the chapter on HOW TO REMEMBER MELODY, melodies can start on any degree of the scale and, sometimes, on accidentals (notes not falling within the tonic scale), so we can't necessarily predict a starting note for any given key. To a lesser extent does this random aspect apply to harmonies, although, as a good tip, whatever harmony we may start on (and normally it's closely related to the tonic on the cycle of fifths), it's pretty certain that we will <u>finish</u> on the tonic chord. We each have our different ways of remembering the starting note

47

of G, so now listen to it played together with a chord of G7 and play the sequence G7 to C. G7 C is known as the 'perfect cadence', and this example gives us the opportunity to realise that we start our tune NOT on a stable chord of C, but on the unstable G7 that precedes C on the cycle of fifths. Now that the initial harmony of G7 is established in your memories, 'hear' the G melody note then count up to the upper tonic C via the degrees of the scale (5 6 7 8 - G to upper C) and downwards (5 4 3 2 1 - G to lower C). Keep practising this method so that when you reach more complex tunes, you have a method to support your recall of the starting note.

HARMONIC PRINCIPLES ILLUSTRATED

CYCLE OF FIFTHS	SIGNIFICANT BASS MOVEMENT	MOVING INTERNAL HARMONY	CHANGE OF TONALITY
√			

Here we have as basic a harmonic movement as you could wish to meet: just the tonic chord of C and the chord one degree clockwise on the cycle of fifths, G7. Simple as it may appear with only one chord change every two bars, nevertheless take it slowly to start with and develop the sense of 'hearing' where each alternate G7 and C chord fits in with the melody. Although it's early days, you will gradually develop an 'ear' for melody and a separate 'ear' for harmonic sequences and then you will instinctively recognise when chords need to change to support the melody.

MEMORY JOGGERS

ORGANISATION OF SECTIONS	
REPETITION (sections/lines melody/sequence)	√
MATCHING CHORDS TO MELODY NOTES	√
"RECOGNITION" NOTES	
"RECOGNITION" CHORDS	
FINGERING	√
LYRICS	
"HEARING" THE SOUND	√
ASSOCIATION WITH OTHER SONGS	

The attraction of this children's jingle is that the melodic movement is minimal (just two notes drawn from chords of G7 and C) and these right hand chords are 'mechanically' predictable in the way they move on the white notes. We have got to rise above the child's interpretation, though, so let's remember through understanding rather than by reproducing the tune 'mechanically'. When you play the chords in your right hand the melody note is, 99% of the time, the highest note, so by playing just the upper note, you will remember the pure melody. The next item to understand is that the note that falls beneath the melody in each right hand chord is a harmony note and, as such, it must be a component of the harmony indicated in the chord instruction printed over the stave. The chord of G7 is composed of notes G B D F and the chord of C is simply the major triad C E G, so notice how the notes chosen to harmonise with each melody note in the right hand are compatible with those indicated in the chord instruction. As a general tip, when we match melody (and also, in this instance, harmony) notes to the indicated chord, we must do it at that part of the bar where the emphasis falls. The emphasis, or 'stress', could well be at the start of a bar or at the end of a phrase, or at a particular part of the lyric. This means that on our way to the focal point, we are allowed to retain the indicated harmony whilst we play 'passing' notes, which are just incidental notes that link up the more important ones. In practical terms, then, don't look questioningly at each and every 'passing' note for harmonic compatibility - it's the 'emphasis' notes that will conform to the chord and, in this instance, these are the notes that fall on beat 1 of each bar. Remember the right hand two note chords mechanically by all means, but now that you see the principles behind the choice of notes, you will reinforce your remembrance of this jingle through understanding.

Another first principle here is the observation that we just cannot get away with different fingering every time otherwise we are bound to falter sooner or later. We must approach the topic of fingering sensibly and logically. Ignoring the fact that your 4th and 5th fingers are probably less agile than 1 2 & 3, it makes sense when you approach fingering, to lay your hands over the keys - in this case, rest your hands over an octave, thumb on the lower C and 5 on the upper C. You'll see now that the suggested fingering is logical to avoid your fingers finishing up like the roots of an old oak tree! That's enough for this one. True - there are about six pieces called CHOPSTICKS, but this basic 16 bar section is ideal for our purposes.

3. Happy Birthday To You

by Patty S. Hill and
Mildred J. Hill

SUGGESTED CHORD INVERSIONS					
B♭	F B♭ D	F	F A C	C7	G B♭ C E

You have time to prepare yourself for Christmas, Goodnight and New Year's Eve songs, but requests for a Birthday song have a habit of catching you unawares so into the memory, as a matter of priority, it must go. Just 8 bars long and containing only three chords, what could be simpler?

STRUCTURE				
WRITTEN KEY	STARTING/LEAD-IN NOTE	CHORD	TEMPO/RHYTHM	ORGANISATION OF SECTIONS
F	C	C7	3/4 ♩ 112	A

The 8 bars are sub-divided into 4 similar phrases as denoted by the phrasing lines, each with similar, repetitive timing. Once we have examined the piece in detail and feel that we understand it, then it will be much easier to remember it. Consider first the time signature – waltz time 3/4 – because that is what gives 'form' to the succession of melody notes. 3/4 waltz time means that the accent normally falls on the first beat of the bar, so relate the accent on the melody to that of the lyrics, i.e. Happy|Birthday to|You. Next observe the two lead-in notes, which means that we start just before the double bar line. Why do we have 'lead-in' notes here? Because the accents fall on the first beat of the bar in 3/4 time (think of the drummer's bass drum) and as our first accent here is on 'Birthday', we start with lead-in notes which are weaker in emphasis, but guide our ears and our singers' voices to bar no.1. It's just like threading a needle with a weaker piece of thread first. The melody notes of C together with the chord of C7 are important to allow our ears to prepare for a tonality of F, so remember to play that guiding C7 first of all for the lead-in harmony.

HARMONIC PRINCIPLES ILLUSTRATED			
CYCLE OF FIFTHS	SIGNIFICANT BASS MOVEMENT	MOVING INTERNAL HARMONY	CHANGE OF TONALITY
√			

Just three chords necessary, Bb F C7 and each time we move away from F, our key chord, back we come again. Remember these three chords by imagining yourself on a tight piece of elastic. You can move away from F on either side of the cycle by only one degree before the elastic pulls you back home again! You'll soon recognise when a change of harmony is required, so develop your ears to help your memory decide which side of F on the cycle of fifths you should move. Any tip is valid to help your memory at this stage, so lay the chords out in the following way and remember the symmetry:

$$\boxed{F}\;\boxed{C7}\;\boxed{F} - \boxed{F}\;\boxed{Bb}\;\boxed{F} - \boxed{F}\;\boxed{C7}\;\boxed{F}$$

Now that's interesting in bar 7, isn't it? Two chord changes in one bar.

MEMORY JOGGERS	
ORGANISATION OF SECTIONS	
REPETITION (sections/lines melody/sequence)	
MATCHING CHORDS TO MELODY NOTES	√
"RECOGNITION" NOTES	
"RECOGNITION" CHORDS	
FINGERING	
LYRICS	√
"HEARING" THE SOUND	√
ASSOCIATION WITH OTHER SONGS	

In our first example, the NON-MUSICIAN'S JINGLE, we referred to the importance of composing yourself before you start to play so that you are confident and accurate. If you are unsure of these lead-in notes of C, then jog your memory by using the procedure for working out which degree of the scale they fall on. (Page 12 in HOW TO REMEMBER MELODY). Don't worry too much about it here since we will mention this memory jogging idea again in the next example. Traditionally we're in the key of F (to enable singers to deliver their words comfortably between the notes of low C and high C) and from our knowledge of the F scale (see page 33) we would expect to meet a Bb somewhere along the way. This we do in bar 6, so prepare yourself for it, as it is interesting to watch people trying to remember melodies, steadfastly refusing to recognise and play the black notes!

One interesting point concerning the matching of chords to melody is that in this instance the emphasis (apart from the natural one occurring at the start of each bar) falls at the end of each phrase, so that if your memories are building up by relating chords to melody notes then the stronger, emphasised note at the phrase end is the note to concentrate on. Observe the compatibility between the C E & G melody notes with C7, the F melody note with F chords and the D melody note with a Bb chord. This presumes you have sufficient theory to work out mentally that the C triad is C E G, the F triad F A C and the Bb triad Bb D F. This is all good practice for basic music theory and, in our application, a solid foundation for building up your ability to memorise.

When the big moment arrives, you'll want to make sure your friends sing it in the key of F, so don't remember the tune in a linear way (as one part following another), but provide an introduction by playing the last 2 bars, dally on that C7, and wait for the singers to gather impetus into bar 1.

50

STRUCTURE				
WRITTEN KEY	STARTING/LEAD-IN		TEMPO/RHYTHM	ORGANISATION OF SECTIONS
	NOTE	CHORD		
G	B	G	¢ ♩ 96	A B

Without playing a note and without using our memories, let's work out the starting note for the beginning of the chorus where we fit the words 'Jingle Bells'. Sing it to yourself and use this tune as a test-piece to work out which degree of the scale you're on. Count down to the tonic (equivalent to notes B A G) 3 steps on the scale, and you'll find yourself at home on the key note. Soon the idea will become second nature to you as you bring different senses into play, all fusing together to help your memories. (If it helps, many people use the 'floating' tonic sol-fa rather than numbers, in which case you start on ME and count down ME RAY DO.)

We haven't met ¢, split common time, before so just what does this instruction imply over and above 4/4? They both have 4 crotchet beats in the bar but, in practical terms, ¢ implies a minim pulse (two beats to the bar) with the accents falling on beats 1 and 3. Sing JINGLE BELLS quietly and rhythmically and notice how your foot taps twice per bar. In contrast, imagine another Christmas song, WHITE CHRISTMAS, where the 'feel' is definitely 4/4.)

See how the piece splits naturally into Sections A and B, Chorus and Verse, and notice how within each Section lines 1 & 3 and 2 & 4 virtually duplicate each other.

HARMONIC PRINCIPLES ILLUSTRATED			
CYCLE OF FIFTHS	SIGNIFICANT BASS MOVEMENT	MOVING INTERNAL HARMONY	CHANGE OF TONALITY
√			

The harmony is standard, we're in the key of G and we know from the rules of the cycle of fifths that we are likely to meet chords based upon roots of C G D & A, i.e. one degree anti-clockwise from G and one, two or more degrees clockwise. Start to develop the feeling, as you're playing, of sticking very close to the tonic chord of G - as soon as the harmony pulls away from G, it's as if it's on a bit of elastic, and back you go. If we're in the clockwise segment of the cycle, see how useful part of the mnemonic Alsatian Dogs Growl at Cats can be, as when we meet A7 we then remember that we return via a D7 to G.

MEMORY JOGGERS	
ORGANISATION OF SECTIONS	√
REPETITION (sections/lines melody/sequence)	√
MATCHING CHORDS TO MELODY NOTES	√
"RECOGNITION" NOTES	
"RECOGNITION" CHORDS	
FINGERING	√
LYRICS	
"HEARING" THE SOUND	
ASSOCIATION WITH OTHER SONGS	

Any device that helps our memories is valid, so examine the aspect of matching chords to melody notes to see if this approach 'works for you'. Back in CHOPSTICKS, we observed that both harmony and melody notes had to conform to the chord instruction, so now we develop the idea that if the melody note is strong (i.e. not a transient, passing note, but one that falls with emphasis at a significant part of the phrase), then it will be a significant note in the construction of the chord. The major triad of G is G B D, that of C is C E G and, lo and behold, the G chord goes with the B melody in line 1 and the C chord goes with the C melody in line 2! Distinguish between passing notes and 'emphasis' notes: in bar 6 of the chorus notice how the C melody note merely precedes a 'stronger' B note - and this is the one that falls at the end of the phrase and hence is compatible with the G harmony chord. At this early stage, this approach will allow you to develop confidence by providing yet another memory back-up until such time as more musical considerations take over.

A logical and practical fingering pattern is suggested here but if some of the ideas for changing fingers (e.g. 3 2 1) on the same note prove awkward, feel free to stab away with the same finger. Whichever method you use, consistent fingering is important when playing from memory - when you are reading from music you can 'get by' using different fingers every time, but when playing from memory, stumbling over the fingering will throw you.

5. Show Me The Way To Go Home

Words and Music
by Irving King

Show me the way to go home, I'm tired and I want to go to bed, I had a little drink about an hour a-go, And it's gone right to my head. Where ev-er I may roam, On land, or sea, or foam, You can al - ways hear me singing this song, Show me the way to go home.

SUGGESTED CHORD INVERSIONS							
Bb	F Bb D	F	F A C	F7	F A C Eb		
C7	E Bb C	G7	F G B D	Dm	F A D	A7	G A C# E

STRUCTURE				
WRITTEN KEY	STARTING NOTE	LEAD-IN CHORD	TEMPO/RHYTHM	ORGANISATION OF SECTIONS
F	A	F	4/4 ♩ 120	A B

First memorise the lyric - there's no surer way of getting the melody notes right for both pitch, timing and quantity. Timing, of course, is an important subject, so do observe those dotted minims and give them three full 'crotchet' beats.

Let's get the visual presentation right by organising the tune into Sections A and B and once again we see that lines 1 & 3 are similar, as are lines 2 & 4. (We can see that it's just the lyrics that make certain sections busier.) In whichever way you recall the bulk of the tune, if you start inaccurately you'll trip yourself all the way through, so settle yourself, and although you should remember that the key is F, you can take your time and confirm to yourself that the starting note is the third degree of the F scale, A.

Lines 1 & 3 are a trip to the anti-clockwise part of the cycle of fifths, and lines 2 & 4 are a trip to the clockwise part of the cycle of fifths. Notice how the F7 in bar 2 pushes us forward into B♭ in bar 3, and immediately in this tune our attention is held by the feeling of purpose as we move positively from ? to B♭ through bars 1-3. As we revert back to F in bar 4, the tension dissolves and this 4 bar line is then complete. Line 2 provides a gentle trip around the clockwise segment of the cycle of fifths before reaching the tonic chord again at the start of Line 3. An interesting point here, which will enable our ears to assist our memories, is that in line 2 it isn't necessary to make the Dm chord a seventh in order to propel the sequence round the cycle. It doesn't matter if you do - it's just that the sparser flavour of Dm (N.B. the relative minor of F) seems more suitable.

MEMORY JOGGERS	
ORGANISATION OF SECTIONS	√
REPETITION (sections/lines melody/sequence)	√
MATCHING CHORDS TO MELODY NOTES	√
"RECOGNITION" NOTES	√
"RECOGNITION" CHORDS	√
FINGERING	
LYRICS	√
"HEARING" THE SOUND	√
ASSOCIATION WITH OTHER SONGS	

One of the most useful memory joggers of all is the 'odd man out'. If you have a succession of related chords and, all of a sudden, there is an odd one you don't expect, that's the 'recognition' chord that sticks in your memory. We see it here in bar 4 of Section B, the alien A7 that arrives with the word 'foam'. Just a semitone down from B♭ and there you are - unforgettable, isn't it? What of the rest of the chords? How do we remember them? Well, when you've looked at Section A and remembered it, you'll find that Section B is almost the same:

    Section A   F F7 B♭ (F) , F Dm G7 C7
    Section B   F F7 B♭ (A7) , F Dm G7 C7

For the first time in our examples, we now meet accidentals - the notes that don't fall naturally in the scale of F - so the presence of the G♯ 'recognition' notes is going to ring a bell with you when you play the tune from memory.

All that remains now is a procedure for practice. Play each 2 bar phrase separately, making sure that you sing along to get pitch and phrasing correct and when the 2 bar sections are half committed to memory, link them up to make a line at a time. It's then only a short step to remember each 8 bar Section A and B.

An essential tune for your repertoire and useful in the sense that it introduces you, for the first time, to the aspect of 'recognition' (odd man out) chords and 'recognition' notes. Now that we've reached our fifth example, you'll see that the examples are structured and gradually introduce significant points for your memories to focus upon while, at the same time, your hard work is not wasted since ultimately these Special Occasion tunes do need to be remembered. Don't forget that aspect of relating the melody notes to the harmony required - here we could pay particular attention to the B♭ melody notes that go with the B♭ chords and the A melody note being complemented by the odd man out 'recognition' chord of A7.

Learning with the more straightforward tunes will gradually expose you to those areas where you, individually, have difficulty so that you can concentrate on the approach that works successfully for you.

6. Auld Lang Syne

Traditional

SUGGESTED CHORD INVERSIONS							
Bb	F Bb D		F	F A C		C7	G Bb C E
C7	E Bb C	Gm7	F G Bb D	Dm	F A D	A7	G A C# E

You only have to play it once a year, but if 'tonight's the night' and you can't find your music at the crucial moment, let your memory help you see the New Year in.

STRUCTURE				
WRITTEN KEY	STARTING/LEAD-IN		TEMPO/RHYTHM	ORGANISATION OF SECTIONS
	NOTE	CHORD		
F	C	C7	4/4 ♩ 108	A B

As the dancers' arms link up, your memory of a positive C7 to align their voices to the tonality of the key of F will set the ball rolling. C7, the dominant seventh in the key of F, together with a lead-in melody note of C, couldn't be more unambiguous. The tune is organised into two Sections A and B, each consisting of two self-contained lines of 4 bars and you'll notice that the timing is almost identical for the first three bars in every line.

55

HARMONIC PRINCIPLES ILLUSTRATED			
CYCLE OF FIFTHS	SIGNIFICANT BASS MOVEMENT	MOVING INTERNAL HARMONY	CHANGE OF TONALITY
√			

We stick to predictable cycle sequences through-out and we notice that the chord sequence of Section A is repeated exactly in Section B, which must be good news for our severely taxed memories! We've got a few interesting points to focus upon here which will enable us to support our memory processes via understanding. Line 1 (and also line 3) is the same trip either side of the cycle that you first met in HAPPY BIRTHDAY TO YOU, so that will hold no problems for you. You will also remember from the THEORY REVISION chapter that when we move to the point one degree anti-clockwise on the cycle (F to B♭), the B♭ is almost never a 7th; it may possibly move to a minor feel, but normally it's just a plain, major chord. Line 2 illustrates two principles for our memories to focus upon. First the movement from F to Dm: it's a cast out around the cycle from F to D but the absence of the 7th makes the sequence sound a bit 'hymn' like (you don't get many 7ths in hymns!). Just as in SHOW ME THE WAY TO GO HOME, you could put the 7ths in if you liked, but it's preferable to remember it as a plain Dm so that your ears and memory get used to an uncluttered harmony. The second point to notice

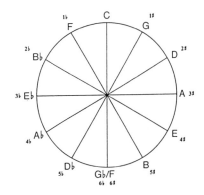

in this line is the interesting way we interrupt our cycle progression to 'cast out' again before reeling in in a steady cycle manner. F – cast out – |Dm|Gm7| – cast out again – |A7|Dm|Gm7|C7|F| . The A7 isn't a 'recognition' chord here like it was in the previous example because here it is part of a closely related sequence.

MEMORY JOGGERS	
ORGANISATION OF SECTIONS	√
REPETITION (sections/lines melody/sequence)	√
MATCHING CHORDS TO MELODY NOTES	√
"RECOGNITION" NOTES	
"RECOGNITION" CHORDS	
FINGERING	
LYRICS	
"HEARING" THE SOUND	√
ASSOCIATION WITH OTHER SONGS	

You'll see here that a knowledge of chord construction really does help your memory – note how the F chords go with an F or C note, the C7 chords go with a C or G note and the B♭ chord goes with a D note. Once again we see the importance of organising the music into a size and format that is understandable. Remember line 1 is a trip either side of F on the cycle, line 2 has our two 'cast outs', the second one reminding us of our mnemonic Alsatian Dogs Growl at Cats, leading home to F. You're now ready for a public performance until your nerve deserts you on the morning of 31st December!

7. The Anniversary Waltz

Words and Music
by Dave Franklin and Al Dubin

Tell me I may al - ways dance the An-ni-ver-sa-ry Waltz with you; Tell me this is real ro - mance, An An-ni-ver-sa-ry dream come true. Let this be the an-them to our fu - ture years, To mil-lions of smiles and a few lit - tle tears. May I al - ways list - en to the An-ni-ver-sa-ry Waltz with you.

SUGGESTED CHORD INVERSIONS

F	F A C	C	G C E	C7	E B♭ C	G7	F G B D	G7+	F B D♯
Gm7	F G B♭ D	D7	F♯ A C D	Dm7	F A C D	A7	G A C♯ E	C♯°	G B♭ C♯ E

STRUCTURE

WRITTEN KEY	STARTING/LEAD-IN NOTE	CHORD	TEMPO/RHYTHM	ORGANISATION OF SECTIONS
C	C	C	3/4 WALTZ ♩ 104	A₁ A₂ B A₃

How should we analyse this tune? It's romantic and leisurely; it's a dance, so we must remember it well enough to play it fluently at the correct dance tempo. This is our first full 32 bar piece, which we subdivide into 4 sections of 8 bars, for convenience A₁ A₂ B A₃. There is good reason for this, as it will prepare your memory for evergreens such as QUANDO QUANDO which consist of 4 Sections AABA where all the A's are the same. Our A's aren't quite the same here, but they differ only slightly.

HARMONIC PRINCIPLES ILLUSTRATED

CYCLE OF FIFTHS	SIGNIFICANT BASS MOVEMENT	MOVING INTERNAL HARMONY	CHANGE OF TONALITY
√	√		

View the piece in its entirety to develop the concept of 'form' and 'shape' and so that you can see each line in context. Start with the Intro and observe that even this has a lead-in note. As this line is a 'pinch' from the last 4 bars, it doesn't even start on the tonic but it does follow the cycle - Dogs Growl at Cats (D7 G7 C). Intros are there to launch us into the body of the tune, so what better chord to precede Section A₁ than the dominant seventh, G7? After the intro, help your memory by looking at similarities in each of the A Sections as regards timing and melody. You'll often see similarities between corresponding sections in parallel melody lines (compare line 1 of Sections A₁ and A₂), or in timing patterns (compare line 2 of Sections A₁A₂A₃). It's here in Section A₁ that we first meet a significant ascending bass line. Don't remember the chords in rote fashion (i.e. without understanding) - they are significant because of the bass movement, C C♯ to D. There will be more examples of this movement in the INTERMEDIATE and ADVANCED SECTIONS to enable us to commit to memory the idea that our minds must look for and focus on bass movement. Since this is our first attempt to memorise this particular sequence (whilst taking note of the concept of a rising bass note) play it repeatedly, in isolation, so that you start to memorise through familiarity with both the notes and chord sequences (practical) and the observation of a rising bass (theoretical). N.B. Diminished chords are useful as 'bridge' or 'link-up' chords since they don't possess a tonality of their own and hence don't disturb the ears of the listeners by pulling them away from the tonality of the written key. When we add a 'seventh' note to a chord, it becomes 'unstable' and wishes to progress to the next point around the cycle, but when we add the augmented fifth as well as the seventh, the chord becomes even more unstable and possesses a 'flavour' of its own. Listen to this in bar 6 of A₂ so that your ears retain the flavour of the G7+ chord.

MEMORY JOGGERS

ORGANISATION OF SECTIONS	
REPETITION (sections/lines melody/sequence)	√
MATCHING CHORDS TO MELODY NOTES	
"RECOGNITION" NOTES	√
"RECOGNITION" CHORDS	
FINGERING	√
LYRICS	
"HEARING" THE SOUND	√
ASSOCIATION WITH OTHER SONGS	

The other application, in this example, of a G7+ chord is to support the 'recognition' melody note of D♯ in the final bar of Section B. (It is the melody note that is significant because it is an accidental - the chord merely adopts a D♯ instead of a D to avoid a clash of harmony.)

If you don't pay attention to the fingering in the early bars, then by the time you hit the sixth successive rising melody note (C D E G A B), you will have run out of fingers. Stick to the finger pattern suggested or remember your own, but either way, you cannot avoid the problem.

8. Spanish Eyes

Words by Charles Singleton
& Eddie Snyder

Music by
Bert Kaempfert

Blue _____ Span-ish eyes _____

Tear drops are falling from your Spanish eyes _____

Please _____ please don't cry _____

This is just a - dios and not good - bye. _____

Soon _____ I'll re - turn _____

Bringing you all the love your heart can hold _____

Please _____ say Si Si _____ Say

you and your Spanish eyes will wait for me. _____

SUGGESTED CHORD INVERSIONS									
C	G C E	Cm	G C E♭	G	G B D	G7	F G B D	D7	F♯ A C D

STRUCTURE				
WRITTEN KEY	STARTING/LEAD-IN		TEMPO/RHYTHM	ORGANISATION OF SECTIONS
	NOTE	CHORD		
G	B	G	₡ BEGUINE ♩ 108	A B

With practice, we extend our non-playing recall to remember written key, starting note and significant 'recognition' chords or melody notes – ones that may otherwise prove to be stumbling blocks. We organise our music so that the total 32 bars are subdivided into two 16 bar Sections A and B. Immediately the similarities between alternate lines are apparent. The timing and phrasing of lines 1 & 3 are virtually identical, as are lines 2 & 4. Thus, when we look for visual similarity, we see that line 3 is the same as line 1, but a tone interval down. (Compare lines 1 and 3 in THE ANNIVERSARY WALTZ for another example of similar melody lines a tone interval apart.) Commit lines 1 and 2 to memory, then, and your work in memorising the remainder is halved.

HARMONIC PRINCIPLES ILLUSTRATED

CYCLE OF FIFTHS	SIGNIFICANT BASS MOVEMENT	MOVING INTERNAL HARMONY	CHANGE OF TONALITY
√			

We look at the chords now in their simplest form and see if we can link them up with our friend, the cycle of fifths. In fact, the complete sequence sticks like glue to the tonic chord of G with first a movement one degree clockwise (G to D7) and then, in Section B, a movement one degree anti-clockwise from G to C. From our knowledge of the rules of the cycle, we know that when we move one degree anti-clockwise on the cycle (in this case G to C) we can change the form of the C chord to introduce variety before returning to the tonic and this we see in Section B where the C chord changes from major to minor.

MEMORY JOGGERS	
ORGANISATION OF SECTIONS	
REPETITION (sections/lines melody/sequence)	√
MATCHING CHORDS TO MELODY NOTES	√
"RECOGNITION" NOTES	√
"RECOGNITION" CHORDS	
FINGERING	
LYRICS	
"HEARING" THE SOUND	
ASSOCIATION WITH OTHER SONGS	

In this piece the chords are very standard, but there are two 'recognition' notes – the E and E♭ corresponding to the chords of C and Cm that fall half way through Section B. Many people (indeed, most people) have only relative pitch so that when a tune leaps upwards by a substantial sixth interval, they have difficulty in determining the note from their sense of relative pitch. As this sixth interval occurs at the climax of the tune, we've got to make sure we remember that high note, or the performance is destroyed! We know the chord following G7 is a C chord and we know the E note is compatible with it, but in whichever way you support your memory of notes and harmony, that 'recognition' climax note of E must be remembered (either musically or unmusically). Once you can remember the E note, the E♭ follows from your sense of relative pitch, and with it, the compatible harmony of Cm.

Once again we can use the memory jogger of understanding the component parts of the chord to assess compatibility with the melody note (e.g. the F natural melody note in the 6th bar of Section B obviously calls out for the G7 chord and the C melody at the end of line 2 of Section A, not being a component of the G chord, reminds us to change to D7).

Now that we have the approach to set about remembering the music and the motivation to succeed, how can we make the tune personal to us, i.e. 'customise' it to suit our ears?

(1) In line 3 of Section A, start on Am7 and within each bar alternate between Am7 and D7 to provide more harmonic interest.

(2) As an introduction to harmony, play Section A in thirds, that is, in addition to the melody note, play the note falling a third interval below in order to harmonise with it.

Music, as always, should be fun and if these hints on customising and adapting to taste appeal to you, you can extend these 'memory' achievements by applying your new learning to other tunes.

9. I Love You Because

Words and Music
by Leon Payne

SUGGESTED CHORD INVERSIONS					
F	F A C	C	G C E	C7	G Bb C E
C°	Gb A C Eb	G7	F G B D	D7	F# A C D

This again, like SPANISH EYES, is a tune for consolidation where we can mark time and gain confidence for the more complex tunes that follow.

STRUCTURE				
WRITTEN KEY	STARTING/LEAD-IN		TEMPO/RHYTHM	ORGANISATION OF SECTIONS
	NOTE	CHORD		
C	G	G7	C = 4/4 FOX ♩ 108	A₁A₂B A₃

As always, you must sing the words so that you consider the tune with 'feeling'. This will help you in timing and interpretation. You must also organise the music into regular A and B type Sections and note the similarities. I LOVE YOU BECAUSE is a gentle, flowing song and, although it is written in 4/4, it still cries out for a 'loping' 2 bass notes to the bar feel. We could indicate this by writing in a ¢ time signature just as we did in JINGLE BELLS. Many people have trouble with their timing, and a typical trap to fall into is to skip a beat on bars 3 & 4 of Section A₁. Since timing and the development of a smooth flow are so important to memory, we have 'counted' the crotchets below the stave. (If you play with a 2/4 pulse, you may prefer to count 1 2 & 3 4 or 1 & 2 &.)

HARMONIC PRINCIPLES ILLUSTRATED			
CYCLE OF FIFTHS	SIGNIFICANT BASS MOVEMENT	MOVING INTERNAL HARMONY	CHANGE OF TONALITY
√			

Examine the chord sequence and you'll notice that we stay very close to the tonic throughout, alternating between trips one degree anti-clockwise on the cycle of fifths C C7 F and one and two degrees clockwise G7 C D7 G7 C , in fact, sequences you have already met in our examples to date. We can use this example to introduce some more 'sounds' to our memories.

(1) Your memories now store the sound of the sequence Dm7 G7 C as an extension to G7 C so insert this in the final 2 bars of A₁ to provide variety.

(2) A cycle movement one degree anti-clockwise can promote a Country & Western flavour so focus upon the sequence C F C in bars 7 & 8 of A₂.

(3) Let's now introduce the sound of the diminished chord as a feature (rather than as a 'bridge' as seen in THE ANNIVERSARY WALTZ) by using C° to provide emphasis in bar 3 of Section B. This doesn't upset our cycle sequence at all, and its use will introduce it to our repertoire of sounds so that when we attempt to memorise tunes such as MY PRAYER and UNFORGETTABLE, it will provide a cross-reference.

MEMORY JOGGERS	
ORGANISATION OF SECTIONS	
REPETITION (sections/lines melody/sequence)	
MATCHING CHORDS TO MELODY NOTES	
"RECOGNITION" NOTES	√
"RECOGNITION" CHORDS	√
FINGERING	
LYRICS	√
"HEARING" THE SOUND	√
ASSOCIATION WITH OTHER SONGS	√

In practical terms, our most valuable memory joggers are the 'recognition' notes and chords. 'Recognition' notes occur if there is a large interval (as in SPANISH EYES) or if there are accidentals, and in Section B the F# accidental pulls our thinking immediately to the D7 chord of which it is a main component. The only 'recognition' chords here are those we could introduce to impart 'flavour' – the C F C Country & Western fill-in and the C° C sequences. Play both these sequences with emphasis in your practice to assimilate their 'sounds' into your repertoire. You'll notice that a fill-in melody sequence is also suggested at the end of Section B to provide a smooth bridge between the melody passages.

10. Gentle On My Mind

Words and Music
by John Hartford

STRUCTURE				
WRITTEN KEY	STARTING/LEAD-IN NOTE	CHORD	TEMPO/RHYTHM	ORGANISATION OF SECTIONS
C	G	G7	¢ FOXTROT ♩ 84	A B C D

Although we have already seen the importance of the 'organisation' of our music into 4 bar lines and self-contained sections, GENTLE ON MY MIND is a perfect example of the need to organise our music since it incorporates two extra 2 bar phrases. The whole tune consists of 2 x 8 bars and 2 x 10 bars - so if you forget the visual layout, then you will have to rely on your memory of the extended lyrics (excluded here for copyright reasons) to pull you through. Now, when you think of the tune, you should automatically say, "Ah yes, an extra 2 bars in Sections C & D". (Always 'associate' points you wish to remember with other things, as you then provide yourself with with a 'hook' to pull the facts from your memory.)

Interpretation, as always, is of paramount importance so imagine Dean Martin singing a 'lazy' 2/4 feel. Think of the idiom 'Li'l ole wine drinker me', so that you recall the correct rhythm, tempo and 'flavour'.

HARMONIC PRINCIPLES ILLUSTRATED			
CYCLE OF FIFTHS	SIGNIFICANT BASS MOVEMENT	MOVING INTERNAL HARMONY	CHANGE OF TONALITY
√		√	

Now that we're 'organised', the harmonic principle that is new to us in this example is the descending internal harmony, C Cmaj7 C6 and Dm Dm(maj7) Dm7 corresponding to moving 'internal' notes C B A and D C♯ C above static bass notes of C and D respectively. Although this is the first time that we've met an internal harmony change, it is extremely common, and it is important for you to be accurate and adopt good musical habits. Get your fingers used to the inversions suggested in the chord grid and the more advanced player may also insert these extra notes in the right hand to fall beneath the melody note. (N.B. Melody must always be the top note played.) Don't forget, it's only hard work the first time you encounter and memorise a new sequence. Once you have the background of the harmonic principles that we are gradually introducing, and the ability to reproduce these 'sounds' and sequences from memory, life will be so much easier when it comes to memorising tunes with similar principles.

MEMORY JOGGERS	
ORGANISATION OF SECTIONS	√
REPETITION (sections/lines melody/sequence)	
MATCHING CHORDS TO MELODY NOTES	
"RECOGNITION" NOTES	√
"RECOGNITION" CHORDS	
FINGERING	
LYRICS	
"HEARING" THE SOUND	√
ASSOCIATION WITH OTHER SONGS	√

Our 'landmarks' then are the 'recognition' sequences of C Cmaj7 C6 and Dm Dm(maj7) Dm7 which are extended in Sections C and D as shown. We remember easily the irregularity of Sections C and D which contain an extra 2 bars each. Once we've reduced the song to basics for ease of understanding so that our memories aren't burdened with a welter of information, can we suggest ways to add interest? Well, lines 2 4 6 & 8 are very bare without some form of filler, so play the suggested extra melody notes that fall in the brackets and, if you like these, then soon they will be remembered by you just as readily as the melody. By playing these repetitive, fill-in lines at the conclusion of each section, we bind the tune together as a whole, helping our memories to link each section together. If you wish to stamp your own personal style on the tune, it may well be that you can remember standard 'filler' sequences so, as a suggestion, in lines 2 & 6 alternate chords Dm7 G7 Dm7 G7 and in line 4 insert the sequence C C6 Cmaj7 C6 . The former you will remember from SPANISH EYES and the latter you will soon meet in BEGIN THE BEGUINE. It just shows you, once you reduce music to small sections and commit them to memory, they crop up everywhere!

11. Kiss Me Honey Honey (Kiss Me)

Words and Music
by Al Timothy & Michael Julian

A CHORUS

Kiss me, honey honey, kiss me. Thrill me, honey honey, thrill me.

Don't care ev-en if I blow my top, But honey honey, don't stop.

B VERSE

I'd like to play a little game with you, A little game especially made for two.

If you come close then I will show you how. Closer, closer now.

A CHORUS

Kiss me, honey honey, kiss me. Thrill me, honey honey, thrill me.

Don't care ev-en if I blow my top, But honey honey, don't stop.

SUGGESTED CHORD INVERSIONS							
B♭	F B♭ D	F	F A C	F7	F A C E♭	C	G C E
C7	G B♭ C E	C7	E B♭ C	G7	F G B D	Gm	G B♭ D

STRUCTURE				
WRITTEN KEY	STARTING/LEAD-IN		TEMPO/RHYTHM	ORGANISATION OF SECTIONS
	NOTE	CHORD		
F	F	F	¢ CHA CHA 𝅗𝅥 63	A B

Just two 8 bar sections – Chorus and Verse – each with a different tonality. The key signature is F, corresponding to the tonality of the chorus, so you would start in this case with the chorus and then alternate between 8 bar sections – chorus/verse/ chorus/verse etc. If you wished, you could preface the start of the tune by playing the last 4 bars of the chorus as an introduction (just as you did for THE ANNIVERSARY WALTZ) which would then add a little 'shape' to the overall presentation. This doesn't require any great feat of memory since you will have to remember the last 4 bars anyway.

HARMONIC PRINCIPLES ILLUSTRATED			
CYCLE OF FIFTHS	SIGNIFICANT BASS MOVEMENT	MOVING INTERNAL HARMONY	CHANGE OF TONALITY
√			√

This example is a perfect vehicle to introduce our memories to a change of tonality, in this case changing from F to C as we go from chorus to verse. (Your mind is now prepared for tonality changes in tunes like YELLOW SUBMARINE.) The verse presents no memory difficulties, possessing just the tonic chord C and its dominant 7th, G7, and the chorus is only slightly more complex as it moves either side of the tonic according to the rules of the cycle of fifths – just as we first met in HAPPY BIRTHDAY TO YOU.

MEMORY JOGGERS	
ORGANISATION OF SECTIONS	
REPETITION (sections/lines melody/sequence)	√
MATCHING CHORDS TO MELODY NOTES	√
"RECOGNITION" NOTES	√
"RECOGNITION" CHORDS	
FINGERING	
LYRICS	
"HEARING" THE SOUND	
ASSOCIATION WITH OTHER SONGS	

It is interesting to note that we retain the key signature of F throughout with the result that when we play the verse, which has a tonality of C, each time we encounter the note of B, it has to have a natural sign before it to be compatible with the key signature of F. If you look at the notes of the bars that contain the B natural, you'll see that they consist of notes drawn from the arpeggio of G7 – another example of matching melody notes to the desired harmony. Similarly in bar 6 of the chorus, the notes of D B♭ G are the three components of the Gm harmony.

When we introduce a tune, in order to align our ears to the written key, we may always play a dominant seventh to start, e.g. as when we introduced HAPPY BIRTHDAY TO YOU. Following on from this, we now observe that we can effect a smooth transition from verse to chorus to verse by bridging the gap with the dominant seventh appropriate to each following section. First your memory must recall that the sections alternate between tonalities of F C F and then they must extend this to allow you to preface each section with the appropriate lead-in chord – your first steps in modulation.

TABULATION OF HARMONIC PRINCIPLES ILLUSTRATED IN BASIC SECTION

EXAMPLE	TITLE	HARMONIC PRINCIPLES ILLUSTRATED			
		CYCLE OF FIFTHS	SIGNIFICANT BASS MOVEMENT	MOVING INTERNAL HARMONY	CHANGE OF TONALITY
1	THE NON-MUSICIAN'S JINGLE				√
2	CHOPSTICKS	√			
3	HAPPY BIRTHDAY TO YOU	√			
4	JINGLE BELLS	√			
5	SHOW ME THE WAY TO GO HOME	√			
6	AULD LANG SYNE	√			
7	THE ANNIVERSARY WALTZ	√	√		
8	SPANISH EYES	√			
9	I LOVE YOU BECAUSE	√			
10	GENTLE ON MY MIND	√		√	
11	KISS ME HONEY HONEY	√			√

INTERMEDIATE SECTION

EXAMPLE	JINGLES	SONGS FOR SPECIAL OCCASIONS	EVERGREENS/ STANDARDS	PRACTICE OR PARTY PIECES
12		WE'LL MEET AGAIN		
13		I DO LIKE TO BE BESIDE THE SEASIDE		
14			SATIN DOLL	
15			LOVE ME TENDER	
16			MISTY	
17			BEGIN THE BEGUINE	
18			I COULD HAVE DANCED ALL NIGHT	
19				THE ENTERTAINER
20				EL CUMBANCHERO

12. We'll Meet Again

Words and Music
by Hugh Charles & Ross Parker

We'll meet a - gain, don't know where, don't know when, But I know we'll meet a-gain some sunny day.

Keep smil-ing thro', just like you al - ways do, Till the blue skies drive the dark clouds far a- way. So will you

please say hello to the folks that I know, Tell them I won't be long, They'll be happy to know that as you saw me go, I was singing this song.

We'll meet a - gain, don't know where, don't know when, But I know we'll meet a-gain some sunny day.

SUGGESTED CHORD INVERSIONS					
C	G C E	G	G B D	G7	F G B D	D7	F♯ A C D
A7	G A C♯ E	Am7	G A C E	E7	G♯ B D E	B7	F♯ A B D♯

Goodnight celebrations tend to linger on, so rather than play SHOW ME THE WAY TO GO HOME twice, WE'LL MEET AGAIN is a nice schmaltzy foxtrot to memorise and thereby astound those revellers who are taking notice!

STRUCTURE

| WRITTEN KEY | STARTING/LEAD-IN | | TEMPO/RHYTHM | ORGANISATION OF SECTIONS |
	NOTE	CHORD		
G	D	G	$\frac{4}{4}$ ♩ 112	A₁A₂B A₂

This is an AABA type format with the expected change of tonality in Section B. We're going to memorise the tune in the key of G so that the singers are not unduly stretched on the high notes (i.e. not rising above top C or D). However, as we memorise in this book via understanding, you may readily, if you wish, transpose up and memorise the tune in B♭. The principles are the same, you just sing a minor third higher and, in the process, develop an ability to transpose.

HARMONIC PRINCIPLES ILLUSTRATED

CYCLE OF FIFTHS	SIGNIFICANT BASS MOVEMENT	MOVING INTERNAL HARMONY	CHANGE OF TONALITY
√			

In normal circumstances, this is about as far as you will cast out around the cycle of fifths. Casting out 4 degrees from the tonic chord of G brings us to B7 and thereafter we travel back home via each intervening point on the cycle. Part of our long mnemonic for remembering the sequence of keys is Boys Extra Appetite During Games to represent the root notes of B E A D G (even think of the word BEAD to jog your memory). By musical or unmusical means we have to remember this sequence, but don't try to remember the number of bars associated with each chord, since it is more musical to refer to the MEMORY JOGGERS section and see how to match the harmony to the melody.

When we come to Section B, the Middle Eight Section, we take a little trip one degree anti-clockwise on the cycle | G | G7 | C | before giving ourselves 4 bars (the latter half of Section B) to prepare for the G chord at the start of the final Section A₃, and what better lead-in than the two preceding points on the cycle, A and D?

MEMORY JOGGERS

ORGANISATION OF SECTIONS	
REPETITION (sections/lines melody/sequence)	
MATCHING CHORDS TO MELODY NOTES	√
"RECOGNITION" NOTES	√
"RECOGNITION" CHORDS	
FINGERING	
LYRICS	
"HEARING" THE SOUND	√
ASSOCIATION WITH OTHER SONGS	√

We extend our memory of the title to include key, starting note, etc. and in the same flash of recall we know that WE'LL MEET AGAIN is a tune conforming to the cycle of fifths. What is interesting for us and our memories is the way the harmonies change form to match the melody notes. The second bar includes a significant 'recognition' note of D♯ (not E♭ but D♯ – think of accidentals here as sharps, since we are in a 'sharp' key) and we know that the harmony must move away from G, but how far around the cycle should we go? It's not until we get past the D, the A and the E chords that we reach the root of B whose major chord does contain that significant note of D♯. If our memories fail us for this second chord, then our knowledge of chord construction will save the day. Thereafter we use a combination of 'ears' and memory of the cycle sequence to keep our harmonies matched to the melody. Look at the second line of Section B, the Middle Eight, and notice how you change from the brighter feel of A7 to the more mellow flavour of Am7 before returning to G via the obligatory dominant seventh chord of D7.

Now that this extended cycle sequence is in your memory, you could cross refer, and cope quite happily with these songs:

TITLE	WRITTEN KEY	SEQUENCE IN WRITTEN KEY				
WHO'S SORRY NOW	B♭	D7	G7	C7	F7	B♭
FIVE FOOT TWO	C	E7	A7	D7	G7	C
THE CHARLESTON	B♭	D7	G7	C7	F7	B♭
I GOT RHYTHM (MIDDLE 8)	B♭	D7	G7	C7	F7	B♭

13. I Do Like To Be Beside The Seaside

by John A. Glover-Kind

SUGGESTED CHORD INVERSIONS

E♭7	G B♭ D♭ E♭		B♭		F B♭ D		F		F A C	
F7	F A C E♭	C7	G B♭ C E	C7	E B♭ C	G7	F G B D	Gm	G B♭ D	
Gm7	F G B♭ D	D7	F♯ A C D	Am7	G A C E	E7	G♯ B D E	F♯°	F♯ A C D♯	

STRUCTURE

WRITTEN KEY	STARTING/LEAD-IN NOTE	CHORD	TEMPO/RHYTHM	ORGANISATION OF SECTIONS
F	C	C7	6/8 MARCH ♩. 120	A B A C

It's a jaunty little march in a triplet 6/8 feel. (Think of the march BLAZE AWAY for a similar feel, rather than COLONEL BOGEY which is still a march but in 2/4). Set the mood with the written intro or any other of your choice, so long as you remember to preface the main body of the tune with the lead-in notes of C and C♯, corresponding to the lyrics, "Oh, I...".

HARMONIC PRINCIPLES ILLUSTRATED

CYCLE OF FIFTHS	SIGNIFICANT BASS MOVEMENT	MOVING INTERNAL HARMONY	CHANGE OF TONALITY
√	√		

This is strictly a cycle of fifths tune, the principles of which are now firmly established in our memories. However, in addition, it contains two useful harmonic devices that we can memorise easily in this tune and then recall by cross reference as and when necessary. We know from the cycle rules that we may move one degree anti-clockwise, but the rules don't tell us how to get back on to the cycle in order to return to the tonic. One device for doing this which really must be memorised as it crops us so frequently, is the one we see at the end of Section A - B♭ to its relative minor Gm via D7. Let's prepare our minds like this:

(1) We're in F and we've gone one degree anti-clockwise to B♭.

(2) B♭ has a close affinity in sound with its relative minor Gm (NOT Gm7).

(3) Gm is just two steps away from the tonic of F via the cycle, and therefore provides a route home.

(4) D7 isn't related to B♭, but it is the obvious choice to precede Gm as we can see from the cycle.

Put it all together and we arrive at the mini-sequence B♭ D7 Gm , so play this repeatedly to memorise the 'sound' of the sequence and see how often you recognise it now as a filler sequence in tunes such as IT'S A SIN TO TELL A LIE and I'M GONNA SIT RIGHT DOWN AND WRITE MYSELF A LETTER. (THERE'S A KIND OF HUSH actually uses this sequence for the first 3 bars.) Let's call this sequence the 'Blackpool Tower' sequence for its ready application in bright and breezy tunes.

MEMORY JOGGERS

ORGANISATION OF SECTIONS	√
REPETITION (sections/lines melody/sequence)	
MATCHING CHORDS TO MELODY NOTES	
"RECOGNITION" NOTES	
"RECOGNITION" CHORDS	√
FINGERING	
LYRICS	
"HEARING" THE SOUND	√
ASSOCIATION WITH OTHER SONGS	√

Now that this commonly encountered sequence is committed to memory, let's look at the second harmonic device, the 'recognition' chord E♭7 in Section B. Just as we have seen diminished chords used as 'bridge' chords, so we may sometimes see a chord such as this E♭7 acting as a bridge. How do we remember it? Well, think of it as lying just a semitone above the D7 that you're about to play and remember that a pleasing 'device' in music is to slide down to the chord you want via the chord lying a semitone above it. (We actually see this in a somewhat slower setting in our next example, SATIN DOLL - bars 6 & 7 of Section A.) Although the E♭7 to D7 movement does represent a pleasing harmonic device, and you will meet this often in arrangements, when the E♭7 provides a bridge we must remember the sound of the pedal/bass movement, in this case descending from F to D via E♭. For the first time we can investigate a situation where the bass movement is of paramount importance, with the E♭7 chord merely following the bass progression.

14. Satin Doll

Words by Johnny Mercer

Music by Duke Ellington & Billy Strayhorn

SUGGESTED CHORD INVERSIONS								
D♭7	F A♭ B D♭	A♭m7	G♭ A♭ B E♭	F	F A C	C	G C E	
C7	E B♭ C	G7	F G B D	Gm7	F G B♭ D	D7	F♯ A C D	
Dm7	F A C D	A7	G A C♯ E	Am7	G A C E	Em7	G B D E	

"... ♪ speaks Latin, ♪ that Satin Doll 2 3 4, 1 2 3 4." No room for your memories to falter here, with this steady 4 in the bar pulse, or the thread will be lost.

STRUCTURE				
WRITTEN KEY	STARTING/LEAD-IN NOTE CHORD		TEMPO/RHYTHM	ORGANISATION OF SECTIONS
C	A	Dm7	C = 4/4 FOX ♩ 112	A A B A

Once again it's AABA with the usual change of tonality in Section B. Notice that where there are gaps at the end of phrases, suggested bass patterns are notated to the right to give your memory the opportunity to 'hear' and recall bass notes which, after the melody notes, are the most important notes in your music.

HARMONIC PRINCIPLES ILLUSTRATED			
CYCLE OF FIFTHS	SIGNIFICANT BASS MOVEMENT	MOVING INTERNAL HARMONY	CHANGE OF TONALITY
√			

This time we are still comforted by an overall adherence to the cycle principles, but just look at the way we take a 2 bar melody phrase in line 1 (a 'motif'), play it, move it all up a tone and play it again. | Dm7 | G7 | Dm7 | G7 | then | Em7 | A7 | Em7 | A7 |. We then reverse this fascinating 'device' by taking the same 'motif', repeating it with a harmony that is lowered one semitone before dropping down to the tonic chord of C from the D♭7 above. (Do you remember in our last example, I DO LIKE TO BE BESIDE THE SEASIDE, we first met the idea of reaching the chord we wanted via the one a semitone above it?) Remembering this in theory is one thing, but in practice you only have to move a semitone away from a 'friendly' key and you are in the wilderness, so practise the A♭m7 to D♭7 sequence, become familiar with it, and it will be useful groundwork for when you play in the key of E♭.

Here, now, is another interesting musical 'device' for your ears and memories to focus upon. We know from the cycle rules that we are normally allowed to travel anti-clockwise from the tonic by one degree, but although the cycle rules say where we should finish, they don't say where we should start! This means that instead of a bald | C | C7 | to F we may effect a smoother transition by using the extended sequence | Gm7 | C7 | F |, and this we see at the start of Section B. Notice how at the end of Section B we prepare for G7 by inserting a Dm7. A 'smooth' device, and now that your attention is drawn to it, you'll remember and recognise it as it occurs.

MEMORY JOGGERS	
ORGANISATION OF SECTIONS	
REPETITION (sections/lines melody/sequence)	√
MATCHING CHORDS TO MELODY NOTES	√
"RECOGNITION" NOTES	
"RECOGNITION" CHORDS	√
FINGERING	
LYRICS	
"HEARING" THE SOUND	√
ASSOCIATION WITH OTHER SONGS	√

The most memorable features of the tune are the cycle chords of | Dm7 | G7 | moving up a tone to | Em7 | A7 | and, similarly, | Am7 | D7 | dropping down a semitone to | A♭m7 | D♭7 |. In each case the melody notes are compatible with the chords (a chicken and egg situation), so that either the chords or melody notes may jog your memory. Pedal sequences are written in to fill the gaps by way of contrast and these you must try to remember as a 'bass' melody line in their own right, not as root notes for a succession of chords. The | A♭m7 | D♭7 | sequence is alien to the key of C, so we consider these to be 'recognition' chords. Study this sequence well because it will then be familiar to you when we come to remember MISTY (example 16) which is in the key of E♭.

74

15.

Love Me Tender

Words and Music
by Elvis Presley and Vera Matson

SUGGESTED CHORD INVERSIONS									
C	G C E	Cm	G C E♭	G	G B D	G7	F G B D	D7	F♯ A C D
A7	G A C♯ E	E7	G♯ B D E	Em	G B E	B7	F♯ A B D♯	Bm7⁻⁵	F A B D

If you can remember these two 8 bar sections via understanding rather than constant 'unreasoning' practice, then you can consider yourself 90% on the road to success. All that remains after this is to tackle the 'variety' that you are likely to meet, since your foundations are now laid.

STRUCTURE				
WRITTEN KEY	STARTING/LEAD-IN NOTE CHORD		TEMPO/RHYTHM	ORGANISATION OF SECTIONS
G	D	G	$\frac{4}{4}$ ♩ 84	AB

A deceptive tune since it is by no means as easy to memorise correctly as you would imagine. Just 16 bars for us to study, but containing a wealth of harmonic interest. Although we organise it into 8 bar Sections A and B, notice how lines 1 & 2 are identical and the timing of line 4 is the same as lines 1 & 2 - in fact, almost a condensed version of an AABA format.

HARMONIC PRINCIPLES ILLUSTRATED			
CYCLE OF FIFTHS	SIGNIFICANT BASS MOVEMENT	MOVING INTERNAL HARMONY	CHANGE OF TONALITY
√	√		

Let's deal with Section A first. With all slow tunes it helps to study the lyrics in order to play a sympathetic interpretation. We observe visually that we are in the key of G and that we move just 2 points clockwise on the cycle

| A7 | D7 | G | , but our 'recognition sound' is the A7 that arrives in bar 2. Cross refer this harmonic movement | G | A7 | (relatively the same harmonically as | C | D7 | or | F | G7 |) to the opening bars of CHANSON D'AMOUR, THE GIRL FROM IPANEMA and SOLITAIRE. Pick these tunes out and memorise the sound of your 'displacement from the tonic'.

When we reach Section B, we can recognise two old friends from I DO LIKE TO BE BESIDE THE SEASIDE:
(1) The movement from a major chord to its relative minor which was | Bb | D7 | Gm | in I DO LIKE TO BE BESIDE THE SEASIDE and here is | G | B7 | Em | , and
(2) The device of inserting a 'bridging' chord - | F | Eb7 | D7 | in I DO LIKE TO BE BESIDE THE SEASIDE and here | G | Bm7-5/F | E7 | .

Let's understand Section B in its entirety first before we confuse the issue by inserting extra sequences. After the | G | B7 | Em | sequence, we conform to the cycle by moving one point anti-clockwise, | G | C | , change the C to Cm (just as we saw in SPANISH EYES), return to G before casting out around the cycle in the normal way, returning to the tonic G chord in the final bar. Now that the overall shape is clear, we introduce 'flavour' first by our 'Blackpool Tower' sequence | G | B7 | Em | which is G to its relative minor and then, in line 4, the descending root note 'bridging' between G and Em. The only niggle our memories might have is, "Why isn't the bridging chord of Bm7-5 a straightforward seventh? Well, it could be, if the melody note was compatible with an F7 but it isn't, so although the notation is cumbersome, it is the flavour required and, while we're on the subject, notice how we could just as well represent it as Dm6/F - the same notes (D F A B), but not quite as easy to memorise, since the Bm7-5 chord does precede E7 on the cycle circumference.

MEMORY JOGGERS	
ORGANISATION OF SECTIONS	
REPETITION (sections/lines melody/sequence)	√
MATCHING CHORDS TO MELODY NOTES	
"RECOGNITION" NOTES	
"RECOGNITION" CHORDS	
FINGERING	
LYRICS	√
"HEARING" THE SOUND	√
ASSOCIATION WITH OTHER SONGS	√

It may help our memories to isolate the significant sequences in Section B.
1) The 'Blackpool Tower' sequence | G | B7 | Em |
2) The Spanish Eyes sequence | C | Cm | G |
3) The bridging chord sequence | G | Bm7-5/F | E7 |
Practise these sequences in isolation then savour them in the context of the tune, as the tempo is leisurely, and they will stay in your mind forever.

16. Misty

Music by Erroll Garner

SUGGESTED CHORD INVERSIONS							
Db7	F Ab B Db	Ab	Ab C Eb	Abm7	Gb Ab B Eb	Eb	G Bb Eb
Eb7	G Bb Db Eb	Bb7	Ab Bb D F	Bb7	F Ab Bb D	Bbm7	Ab Bb Db F
F7	F A C Eb	Fm7	F Ab C Eb	C7	E Bb C	Cm7	G Bb C Eb
G7	F G B D	D7	F♯ A C D	Am7	G A C E		

In this example, we introduce a popular 'ballad' key, Eb, familiarising you with its associated chord sequences, and we also see for the first time a movement 2 degrees anti-clockwise on the cycle of fifths (really only an extension of Eb to Ab, but a nice 'sound' to store in your memory).

STRUCTURE				
WRITTEN KEY	STARTING/LEAD-IN NOTE	CHORD	TEMPO/RHYTHM	ORGANISATION OF SECTIONS
Eb	Bb	Bb7	$\frac{4}{4}$ ♩ 72	A₁ A₂B A₃

32 bars reduced to a simple AABA format with only small differences of timing in each A Section (plus a 'bridge' leading us to Section B).

HARMONIC PRINCIPLES ILLUSTRATED			
CYCLE OF FIFTHS	SIGNIFICANT BASS MOVEMENT	MOVING INTERNAL HARMONY	CHANGE OF TONALITY
√			√

Once again, this tune follows cycle principles throughout, but incorporates some extra devices to increase harmonic interest. Just as we saw in SATIN DOLL, when moving to the point one degree anti-clockwise on the cycle, we may preface that chord by not one but two chords, i.e. Eb to Ab may become Bbm7 | Eb7 | Ab .

Although this is not new to us, we see it here in a different key. Now, for the first time, we meet the extension of the cycle rules that allows us to move, in special circumstances, to the point 2 degrees anti-clockwise from the tonic and we do this via harmonies of Abm7 | Db7 - two chords that are now familiar to you as you remember them from their application in SATIN DOLL! After these two principles, which we have already encountered and memorised, we meet up again with the idea that we first saw back in AULD LANG SYNE and I DO LIKE TO BE BESIDE THE SEASIDE where we travelled part way back home via the cycle and then 'cast out' again still further. Examine line 2 of Section A₁ where we have the sequence Eb | Cm7 | Fm7 | Bb7 , but before we can return home to the tonic chord of Eb, we cast out again to G7 | C7 | F7 | Bb7 and thence home to Eb for the start of the next Section A₂.

Section B, the Middle Eight, conforms to the expected change of tonality Bbm7 | Eb7 | Ab but has the additional variety of popping up a semitone from Ab to Am7 for a further hasty change of tonality before bluntly getting back on course for the tonic Eb.

MEMORY JOGGERS	
ORGANISATION OF SECTIONS	
REPETITION (sections/lines melody/sequence)	
MATCHING CHORDS TO MELODY NOTES	√
"RECOGNITION" NOTES	√
"RECOGNITION" CHORDS	
FINGERING	
LYRICS	√
"HEARING" THE SOUND	√
ASSOCIATION WITH OTHER SONGS	√

As soon as you hit the 'recognition' note of Db in bar 2 - a note common to both Bbm7 and Eb7 - you'll fall into a sequence leading to Ab, with further variety being introduced by extending your visit to Ab with chords of Abm7 and Db7. Again, that 'recognition' note of Db pulls us towards an Ab harmony in the Middle Eight and, upping the Db by a semitone to D, pulls everything up a semitone to a chord of Am7 that resolves to D7, and then bluntly to Fm7. Am7 | D7 would resolve more naturally to a Gm harmony but our sense of timing (only 2 bars left in the Middle Eight) overrides the more graceful resolution to Gm and therefore we abruptly change harmonic direction back to Eb via Fm7 and Bb7.

We meet for the first time several groups of crotchet triplets ⌐3⌐ ♩♩♩, not an easy timing to interpret in allowing each note equal value, but singing and 'leaning on' the lyrics is of the greatest help. Hard work, perhaps, but if you are now thoroughly familiar with the key of Eb, you have at your fingertips the facility of memorising other Eb ballads (of which there are many) with ease.

17. Begin The Beguine

Words & Music by Cole Porter

SUGGESTED CHORD INVERSIONS									
Ab	Ab C Eb	Eb7	G Bb Db Eb	Bb	F Bb D	Bbm	F Bb Db	F	F A C
F7	F A C Eb	Fm7	F Ab C Eb	C	G C E	C6	A C E	Cmaj7	B C E
Cm	G C Eb	G	G B D	G7	F G B D	D7-9	F# A C Eb	Dm7	F A C D

79

Before attempting to remember a beguine, a helpful preparation is to practise a rhythmic left-hand accompaniment pattern that will become second nature to you. Here is a pattern that you could use in Section A.

STRUCTURE				
WRITTEN KEY	STARTING/LEAD-IN NOTE	CHORD	TEMPO/RHYTHM	ORGANISATION OF SECTIONS
C	C	C	4/4 BEGUINE ♩ 120	A₁ A₂B etc

Space permits us only to look at and memorise two 16 bar sections, so having organised them once again in 4 bar lines and cut out the confusing detail in the written chords, we are now ready to look for new facets of musical interest.

HARMONIC PRINCIPLES ILLUSTRATED			
CYCLE OF FIFTHS	SIGNIFICANT BASS MOVEMENT	MOVING INTERNAL HARMONY	CHANGE OF TONALITY
√		√	√

Whereas Section A embodies principles we have already memorised in tunes such as GENTLE ON MY MIND and SPANISH EYES, Section B is different altogether with its twists and turns of tonality. Bars 1 & 2 though are straightforward.

We recognise straight away that the E♭ melody note in bar 1 signals a Cm chord and thereafter we progress around the cycle of fifths $\boxed{Cm\ F7\ B♭}$, pause for breath and then continue with $\boxed{B♭m\ E♭7\ A♭}$. Our memories then tell us to abandon the cycle 'predictions' (which are relatively 'safe' ground) and trust to our 'ears'. What we need for success is a combination of ears, understanding and memory - three interrelated aspects. The thread running through the final 2 bars of Section B is the chord of G. We approach and reach it three times: (1) via the cycle of fifths $\boxed{D7^{-9}\ G}$, (2) using the semitone drop $\boxed{A♭\ G}$, (3) ascending from Fm7 $\boxed{Fm7\ G}$. We could even remember that we play, in apparently random order, every pedal between F and A natural, so how do we use our 'ears' to assist our memories?

MEMORY JOGGERS	
ORGANISATION OF SECTIONS	
REPETITION (sections/lines melody/sequence)	
MATCHING CHORDS TO MELODY NOTES	√
"RECOGNITION" NOTES	√
"RECOGNITION" CHORDS	√
FINGERING	
LYRICS	
"HEARING" THE SOUND	√
ASSOCIATION WITH OTHER SONGS	√

(a) The tune is dynamic at the point where we leave the A♭ harmony in bar 8 and, as we saw in MISTY, we can raise the tension by moving up a semitone. We know from memory that we are going to hover around the chord of G on a tight piece of elastic, so the logical chord to precede G is a D chord, and when it possesses an E♭ note (as indicated by the melody) it becomes D7⁻⁹ (notes of [D] F♯ A C E♭). Play a simple D pedal if you like which will obviously be compatible, but once your ears enjoy the flavour of the other component notes, A and F♯, as pedals, these will be the ones you remember. You may prefer to remember these two harmonies as F♯°/A and F♯°/F♯ – precisely the same notes.

(b) Our second trip away from G on our piece of elastic in the 'TEMPTATION' sequence where we go up a semitone $\boxed{G\ A♭}$ for dramatic effect, and

(c) To maintain compatibility with the melody notes of A♭ and E♭, we use an Fm7 before returning to G, whereupon adding the seventh (G to G7) leads us back to the tonic chord of C.

Section B is awkward but we can't just sweep it under the carpet, we have to look at it from logical angles that enable our memories to retain the information by a process of understanding, cross reference, basic musical principles and so on. Whichever angle is the one that works for you, it's tremendously satisfying when your recall is accurate and you play the piece fluently.

18. I Could Have Danced All Night

Words by Alan Jay Lerner
Music by Frederick Loewe

SUGGESTED CHORD INVERSIONS

F	F A C	F6	F A C D	C	G C E	C6	A C E	Cmaj7	B C E
G	G B D	G7	F G B D	D7	F♯ A C D	Dm		F A D	
Dm6	F A B	Dm7	F A C	Dm7	F A C D	Dm(maj7)		F A C♯	
Am	A C E	E	G♯ B E	B7	F♯ A B D♯	F♯m7		F♯ A C♯ E	

STRUCTURE

WRITTEN KEY	STARTING/LEAD-IN NOTE	CHORD	TEMPO/RHYTHM	ORGANISATION OF SECTIONS
C	C	n/c	4/4 LATIN ♩ 132	A₁ A₂ B A₃

The introduction to this tune is in fact an arpeggio of the C major chord, to be played out of tempo (observe the ⌒ pause mark) to give dramatic effect. It's not necessarily a dance, so if you feel the need to build Section A₃ to a dramatic climax, put pause signs over the chords in the final bar of Section B.

HARMONIC PRINCIPLES ILLUSTRATED

CYCLE OF FIFTHS	SIGNIFICANT BASS MOVEMENT	MOVING INTERNAL HARMONY	CHANGE OF TONALITY
√		√	√

Memorise Sections A₁ and A₂ by remembering the descending internal harmonies as illustrated in GENTLE ON MY MIND, plus a small cycle of fifths sequence as already seen in SPANISH EYES.

Section B will prove less daunting once we stop to examine it and look for the extra bits of information that provide 'hooks' by which to recall the information from our memories. What we see here are movements to totally unrelated keys, from C to E and then from E to G. In this case, although we may remember the leap of a 'third' interval, the melody notes of E F♯ G♯ & B guide us positively to the key of E, just as the same relative notes of G A B & D guide us to a tonality of G. It's the little bit at the end of Section B that we must now understand, a small harmonic movement suspended over a 'pedal' (sustained) bass note of G that leads us back to the original tonality of C.

Don't memorise chord names but look at the harmony notes instead and see how they move down in thirds underneath a steady melody note of C. If you memorise the sequence of notes first, it will be the 'sound' of the sequence

also that you will store in your mind. Should you then wish to play left hand chords, you will memorise them from observation of your right hand notes. Focus also on the concept of these chords changing above a static bass note of G.

Understanding Section A₃ revolves around 'hearing' and memorising the importance of the bass notes. As we've seen in previous examples, we jog our memories by observing the compatibility of melody notes with the desired harmonies and line 1 of Section A₃ is a good example of this. The desired harmonies stick closely to the tonic C, first C to F and thence to the Dm7 which prepares us for the return again to C. What is more interesting for us is to understand the practical application of 'pedal' (sustained/static) bass in bars 5 6 & 7 of this section. Memorise the sound of the Dm7 sitting on top of a G pedal and notice how your ears are relieved when it finally resolves to the more familiar chord of G7 (for clarity we notate this as Dm7/G but it is also called G11.)

MEMORY JOGGERS

ORGANISATION OF SECTIONS	
REPETITION (sections/lines melody/sequence)	
MATCHING CHORDS TO MELODY NOTES	√
"RECOGNITION" NOTES	√
"RECOGNITION" CHORDS	
FINGERING	
LYRICS	
"HEARING" THE SOUND	√
ASSOCIATION WITH OTHER SONGS	√

We remember the dramatic start with an out-of-tempo arpeggio of C major, followed by two descending internal harmony sequences that we recall by cross reference to GENTLE ON MY MIND. Then we have two changes of tonality where the melody notes guide and support our memories and lead us to keys of E and G, finishing up with a 'static' G bass note before the final resolution to the tonic chord of C.

19. The Entertainer

by Scott Joplin

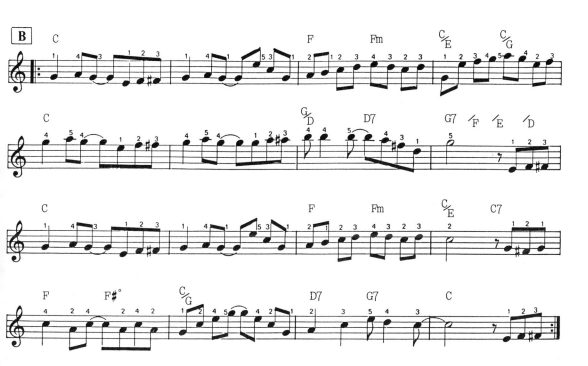

Copyright©1902 by John Stark & Son.

SUGGESTED CHORD INVERSIONS									
F	F A C	Fm	F A♭ C	C	G C E	C7	G B♭ C E	G	G B D
G7	F G B D	D7	F♯ A C D	Am	A C E	F♯°	F♯ A C D♯		

Whatever a 'Ragtime Two Step' was, it certainly wasn't fast, but don't think that makes it any easier to play! Often it's ten times more difficult to play slowly, as the flow must be precise and you just cannot gloss over a mistake. Alternatively referred to as 'The Theme from The Sting', it was composed by Scott Joplin in 1902, so it is important to keep to the original intentions of the composer and the 'flavour' of that era by resisting the temptation to add 6ths and 7ths.

STRUCTURE				
WRITTEN KEY	STARTING/LEAD-IN		TEMPO/RHYTHM	ORGANISATION OF SECTIONS
	NOTE	CHORD		
C	D	G	4/4 ROOK ♩ 100	A A B B etc

The intro is going to be great fun for a 44 note manual – especially as it sounds much better if you play left and right hand in unison. Use the suggested fingering pattern if you wish and use the lower manual when you run out of notes for the third introductory phrase. We only have room for two 16 bar sections here, but these are the most familiar sections. Note that the original tempo was 2/4 but we've rewritten the piece in 4/4 to assist your sight reading.

HARMONIC PRINCIPLES ILLUSTRATED			
CYCLE OF FIFTHS	SIGNIFICANT BASS MOVEMENT	MOVING INTERNAL HARMONY	CHANGE OF TONALITY
√	√		

When you look at the printed copy for this, it is difficult to see the wood for the trees. However, when we strip away the detail that confuses us, what do we see? Once we get to the bones of THE ENTERTAINER'S skeleton, we can reclothe it in a 'period' style. Ragtime pieces are simple in construction and rely heavily on the correct choice of bass notes (imparting that sparse and special 'flavour'),

Line 1 of Section A   C | F | C   +   C | G7 | C

Line 2 of Section A   C | F | Am   +   D7 | G7 | C

Line 3 of Section A   C | F | C   +   C | G7 | C

Line 4 of Section A   C | C7 | F | Fm   +   C | G7 | C

so investigate and memorise the 'sounds' - first the C chord with a C bass, then with an E bass and then with a G bass. Fascinating, isn't it? And with so much more character than a plain C. Use the pedals G A B to 'kick' the tune along at the end of line 2 where we have a natural division half way through Section A. In line 4 of Section A, we see for the first time the use of a descending bass line, lowering tension and leading us gently to a tonic chord of C. (Descending bass lines are a harmonic feature of so many songs - think of IF, FEELINGS, HAPPY HEART, etc.) Here the bass descent isn't chromatic, which in itself would be easy to memorise, but conforms to the component notes of the chord progression C | C7 | F | Fm | C . How do we memorise through understanding? Let's examine this sequence:

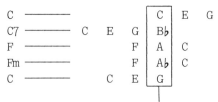

DESCENDING BASS SEQUENCE C B♭ A A♭ G

Now that we have looked at the principles involved, let's see how we can jog our memories when the time comes for a public performance.

MEMORY JOGGERS	
ORGANISATION OF SECTIONS	
REPETITION (sections/lines melody/sequence)	
MATCHING CHORDS TO MELODY NOTES	
"RECOGNITION" NOTES	
"RECOGNITION" CHORDS	√
FINGERING	
LYRICS	
"HEARING" THE SOUND	√
ASSOCIATION WITH OTHER SONGS	

1) The intro is as important as the tune, so think first what note you start on - the second degree of the scale - by laying your hands over the keys and remembering that it's your third finger you need (unless you wish to standardise on alternative fingering). Don't set off too fast and don't play chords on the intro as it is more effective to duplicate the top line an octave below with your left hand.
2) Resist your memory of other songs telling you to play sevenths; your 'visual' memory tells you that the tune is simple with very 'bare' harmonies.
3) When we unclothed the skeleton, the bones of the sequence were C | F | C + C | G7 | C etc. and we reclothed it with chords such as C/E and C/G for the essential 'pedal' flavour.
4) We are aware of the pedal importance rather than the harmony importance and we see 'bridge' pedal sequences of G A B - C half way through Section A and G F E D - C half way through Section B. Additionally we remember the descending pedal sequence in line 4 of Section A from our knowledge of chord construction and when we examine line 4 of Section B, there's a bridge chord of F#° enabling us to return from F to the tonic. Play F | F#° | C/G repeatedly and remember the 'sound'.
5) When we look closely, we remember that whenever pedals have a significant part to play, their movement is restricted to small intervals.

85

20.

El Cumbanchero

Music by Rafael Hernandez

SUGGESTED CHORD INVERSIONS

Ab	Ab C Eb	Eb	G Bb Eb	Bb	F Bb D	Fm	F Ab C
C7	G Bb C E	Cm	G C Eb	Cm+	G# C Eb	Cm6	A C Eb
G7	G B D F	G7	F G B D	Gm	G Bb D	Dm7⁻⁵	F Ab C D

El Cumbanchero

Now that we've reached the end of the INTERMEDIATE SECTION, it's not just a process of memorising, it's accurate recall at speed that counts - a combination of mental and digital dexterity!

STRUCTURE				
WRITTEN KEY	STARTING/LEAD-IN		TEMPO/RHYTHM	ORGANISATION OF SECTIONS
	NOTE	CHORD		
E♭ (Cm)	G	G7	¢ SAMBA 𝅗𝅥 132	A A B A

We see a lot of new features in EL CUMBANCHERO to introduce to our memory store. It is the first time in these graded studies that we meet a tune played in a minor key, but although the tonality is that of Cm, we remember that minor keys have the key signature of their relative major - in this case, E♭. The tune is subdivided into 2 Sections A and B, Section A keeping us firmly anchored on that Cm flavour, whilst in Section B we float away from Cm to effect a temporary change of tonality. Note that sambas have a time signature of ¢, timing written as 4 crotchets per bar but with a pulse of 2 minim beats per bar.

HARMONIC PRINCIPLES ILLUSTRATED			
CYCLE OF FIFTHS	SIGNIFICANT BASS MOVEMENT	MOVING INTERNAL HARMONY	CHANGE OF TONALITY
✓	✓	✓	✓

There is nothing new that we cannot cope with, and what we are doing now is just examining extensions of the principles that we have already memorised elsewhere. Remember that rising internal harmony in BEGIN THE BEGUINE?

Well, in this example the harmony rises and falls chromatically (semitone intervals). This movement provides support and interest underneath a re-petitive melody note. You won't want to concentrate on your left hand as well, so practise this sequence so that your fingers will 'play it for you'.

We first met a descending bass line in THE ENTERTAINER and here, in line 3, we encounter a bass descent adopting the notes from the melodic minor scale. We know that, in order of precedence, the most important notes in our music are first the melody and then the root (or bass) note. Once we remember this descending bass line, the chords simply follow these notes, being compatible with both root and melody. You memory will have to be assisted by plenty of practice, however, if this tune is to get up to tempo.

Focus your mind now on Dm7^{-5} as it is a most important chord in minor applications. Cm has a key signature of E♭, and both Cm and E♭ have scales which include an A♭ note, so we cannot just preface Cm by the usual Dm7 and G7 since the A natural note in Dm7 would clash. We get over this by flattening that fifth note of A to A♭ and calling the chord Dm7^{-5}, so now play the sequence $\boxed{\text{Dm7}^{-5}\;|\;\text{G7}\;|\;\text{Cm}}$ to familiarise your memory with the 'sound of the sequence'.

For our change of tonality (thereby providing harmonic variety in Section B), we have the fairly easy task of memory to recall that we simply move from Cm to C7 at the start of Section B. The C7 leads naturally, according to the cycle rules (page 39) to the Fm chord. Fm6 possesses the same component notes as Dm7^{-5} (F A♭ C D) so we introduce variety in our chord now by switching from an F pedal to a D pedal to use the now familiar sequence $\boxed{\text{Dm7}^{-5}\;|\;\text{G7}\;|\;\text{Cm}}$ to return us smoothly to our initial Cm chord.

MEMORY JOGGERS	
ORGANISATION OF SECTIONS	
REPETITION (sections/lines melody/sequence)	
MATCHING CHORDS TO MELODY NOTES	√
"RECOGNITION" NOTES	
"RECOGNITION" CHORDS	
FINGERING	√
LYRICS	
"HEARING" THE SOUND	√
ASSOCIATION WITH OTHER SONGS	√

We have a firm 2/4 pulse and this is reflected in our two changes of harmony per bar for the first 3 lines of Section A. After the rising internal harmony, we change course completely to follow a descending bass line. Melody and bass lead, with chords following suit, until we meet that well used harmonic device that leads us back to our minor key chord, the $\boxed{Dm7^{-5} \mid G7 \mid Cm}$ sequence.

Section B provides a 'calm' contrast to the busy and repetitive first section.

Note how interest centres on the harmonic support to repetitive melody in Section A, whilst in Section B it is the melody line itself that provides the focal point.

TABULATION OF HARMONIC PRINCIPLES ILLUSTRATED IN INTERMEDIATE SECTION

EXAMPLE	TITLE	HARMONIC PRINCIPLES ILLUSTRATED			
		CYCLE OF FIFTHS	SIGNIFICANT BASS MOVEMENT	MOVING INTERNAL HARMONY	CHANGE OF TONALITY
12	WE'LL MEET AGAIN	√			
13	I DO LIKE TO BE BESIDE THE SEASIDE	√	√		
14	SATIN DOLL	√			
15	LOVE ME TENDER	√	√		
16	MISTY	√			√
17	BEGIN THE BEGUINE	√		√	√
18	I COULD HAVE DANCED ALL NIGHT	√		√	√
19	THE ENTERTAINER	√	√		
20	EL CUMBANCHERO	√	√	√	√

ADVANCED SECTION

EXAMPLE	JINGLES	SONGS FOR SPECIAL OCCASIONS	EVERGREENS/ STANDARDS	PRACTICE OR PARTY PIECES
21		HEARTS AND FLOWERS		
22		THE NATIONAL ANTHEM		
23		THE LONDONDERRY AIR		
24			SUNNY	
25			GEORGIA ON MY MIND	
26			YESTERDAY	
27				THE DAM BUSTERS MARCH
28				AIR ON THE 'G' STRING
29				TICO TICO

21. Hearts And Flowers

by Czibulka-Tobani

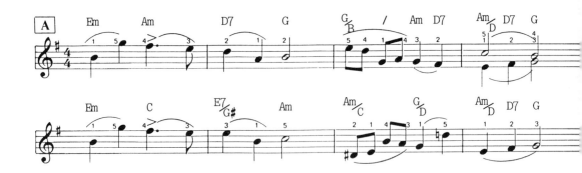

SUGGESTED CHORD INVERSIONS						
C	G C E	G	G B D	D7	F♯ A C D	
Am	A C E	E7	G♯ B D E	Em	G B E	

Take heart, you have only 8 bars to memorise here since these are sufficient to capture the melancholy spirit you wish to represent musically.

STRUCTURE				
WRITTEN KEY	STARTING/LEAD-IN NOTE	LEAD-IN CHORD	TEMPO/RHYTHM	ORGANISATION OF SECTIONS
G	B	Em	4/4 Slow Rock ♩ 63	A

This 8 bar excerpt splits naturally into four 2 bar sections. A mournful 'flavour' demands the use of a minor key, (in this case Em written in its relative major key of G) and notice how the 'flavour' alternates between Em and G. Notice the similarities of timing between bars 1 & 2 and bars 5 & 6.

HARMONIC PRINCIPLES ILLUSTRATED			
CYCLE OF FIFTHS	SIGNIFICANT BASS MOVEMENT	MOVING INTERNAL HARMONY	CHANGE OF TONALITY
√	√		

Look at the similarities between major and minor chords, and notice how we may interchange and adapt them to provide subtleties of 'flavouring'. Specifically, compare phrases 1 & 2 | Em | Am | D7 | and | G/B | Am | D7 | , and phrases 1 & 3 | Em | Am | and | Em | C | .

Initially you may make progress by simply memorising where there is a change of harmony required and then, when your ears become more sophisticated, you will focus on the significant bass note to pull your memory and 'ears' into line. Support your memory by observing that when definite bass notes are specified (e.g. E7/G♯, G/B etc.), these inversions tend to make the harmony more 'unstable' and therefore our ears are unsettled until we move on and resolve to a more stable harmony. We see this clearly in bars 5 & 6 where we meet two unstable sounds, the C chord which supports and F♯ melody (a dissonant sound that propels us forward to a resolution) followed by a further unstable chord of E7/G♯ resolving into the calmer territory of Am.

Do you remember the 'pedal' bass at the conclusion of I COULD HAVE DANCED ALL NIGHT? We meet this principle again in bar 7 but, of course, by now it is in your repertoire and will present no problems of unfamiliarity.

MEMORY JOGGERS	
ORGANISATION OF SECTIONS	
REPETITION (sections/lines melody/sequence)	√
MATCHING CHORDS TO MELODY NOTES	√
"RECOGNITION" NOTES (bass)	√
"RECOGNITION" CHORDS	
FINGERING	
LYRICS	
"HEARING" THE SOUND	√
ASSOCIATION WITH OTHER SONGS	√

Play the bass notes on their own, and you'll discover that they possess a pleasing sequence. Your 'ears' will guide you towards the melody (or, at least, tell you when you are off course), so let your memories focus on the bass movement. Think firstly of the root note and then extend this to remember the chord poised above it. All in all, it is three harmonic trips leading to G.

Yes, we could indeed simplify the harmonies and edit out the harmonic detail that tends to confuse, but with it would go the composer's intentions.

22. The National Anthem

Traditional

SUGGESTED CHORD INVERSIONS							
C	G C E	G	G B D	D	F♯ A D	D7	F♯ A C D
A7	G A C♯ E	Am	A C E	Em	G B E	D♯°	F♯ A C D♯

STRUCTURE				
WRITTEN KEY	STARTING/LEAD-IN NOTE	CHORD	TEMPO/RHYTHM	ORGANISATION OF SECTIONS
G	G	G	3/4 ♩96	A B

We tend to play THE NATIONAL ANTHEM without ever considering that it has a 3 beat to the bar feel which may be represented by either a 3/2 or a 3/4 time signature. Unusually, it is 14 bars long – not that this matters as we consider it merely as two Sections A and B. The key is the important thing because this tune is <u>always</u> played in G, so learn and memorise it in G.

HARMONIC PRINCIPLES ILLUSTRATED			
CYCLE OF FIFTHS	SIGNIFICANT BASS MOVEMENT	MOVING INTERNAL HARMONY	CHANGE OF TONALITY
√	√		

With the wealth of harmony changes and the sparsity of sevenths, it will prove a good introduction to the Ancient and Modern. Boil it down to essentials and you'll see a conformity with the cycle of fifths – chords based on C (one degree anti-clockwise) and E A D G (in the clockwise segment from G). The interesting feature is the way everything dovetails to allow the bass line to provide a contra-melody. Since most organs are restricted to just one octave of pedals, we have to double back on our bass notes to avoid stamping on fresh air, so listen (a) to the melody, (b) to the pedal sequence, and (c) both together. Start to see the tie up with the cycle and see how this type of tune (just as with hymn tunes) takes notes from the chord construction to effect small bass movements – remember we did just the same sort of thing in THE ENTERTAINER. For example, the sequence | G | Am | D | accommodates our pedals by becoming | G | G/B | Am/C | D | and | A7 | D | G | becomes | A7/E | D/F♯ | G | . Notice how we are on a tight bit of elastic that has one end pinned to G – back we come from both sides of the cycle before stretching and casting out again.

Notice and memorise the start of Section B. We have a repetitive melody note of D, the harmony must stay on G, so we 'ring the changes' by playing the component parts of the G triad (G B D) on the pedals. Similarly we harmonise the C melody in bar 3 of Section B by sticking to a D7 and varying the pedal in an ascending fashion. Just to emphasise the contra-melodic nature of the bass line, bars 5 & 6 of Section B incorporate a full descending diatonic scale of G – one that in fact continues its downward path even when the melody (and thus the singers) pause for breath. Finally, we must remember that 'pedal' (static) bass note of D in bar 7.

MEMORY JOGGERS	
ORGANISATION OF SECTIONS	
REPETITION (sections/lines melody/sequence)	
MATCHING CHORDS TO MELODY NOTES	√
"RECOGNITION" NOTES	
"RECOGNITION" CHORDS	
FINGERING	
LYRICS	
"HEARING" THE SOUND	√
ASSOCIATION WITH OTHER SONGS	√

We remember the melody line accurately and when we play the bass line in isolation we discover that that, too, possesses a 'melody' of its own. With these two outside notes determined for us, we may then remember the principles of chord construction to help us recall the chord sequence. We have already met in our studies the use of the diminished chord (in THE ANNIVERSARY WALTZ and I LOVE YOU BECAUSE) and we meet it and savour it in bar 4 of Section A as a 'bridge' chord, bringing us up from G/D to Em.

We remember that the chords stick closely to the cycle rules and we also remember that, being a stately and dramatic tune, it doesn't contain a multitude of sevenths (which would tend to drive us around the cycle in one direction only). We must remember to keep our bass movement small except at the start of Section B when we play the triad notes G B D and D F♯ A for effect, and after the extended descending bass seen in Section B we play two beats of 'pedal' bass before delivery of our monarch safe and sound to the obligatory tonic chord of G.

Don't forget, if you want to reserve your practice time for more popular material, you could always memorise just the first 6 bars of THE NATIONAL ANTHEM. However, it is nice to attempt all 14 bars as you may feel you have an affinity for this more stately type of music.

23. The Londonderry Air

Traditional Irish Air

SUGGESTED CHORD INVERSIONS							
F	F A C	F°	F A♭ B D	C	G C E	C7	G B♭ C E
C7+	G♯ B♭ C E	G	G B D	G7	F G B D	D7	F♯ A C D
Dm	F A D	Dm7	F A C D	Am	A C E	Am7	G A C E

STRUCTURE				
WRITTEN KEY	STARTING/LEAD-IN NOTE	CHORD	TEMPO/RHYTHM	ORGANISATION OF SECTIONS
C	G	G7	$\frac{4}{4}$ ♩ 63	A B

If it wasn't for the complexity of the intro, we would have included this tune in the INTERMEDIATE SECTION. It's structure, then, is an intro, Sections A & B and a small bridge to allow the vocalists to refuel.

HARMONIC PRINCIPLES ILLUSTRATED			
CYCLE OF FIFTHS	SIGNIFICANT BASS MOVEMENT	MOVING INTERNAL HARMONY	CHANGE OF TONALITY
√	√		

The introduction is the really difficult bit, where we need to extend the 'sounds' principles we first learned in THE NATIONAL ANTHEM to provide a basis for our study here. Memory through understanding is easy when the under-standing is easy - but in this case you just have to slowly play these 4 bars again and again to assimilate the 'sounds' in your ears. Just as we remember an apparently illogical sequence of right hand notes as a melody, so now we must develop our store of harmonic 'sounds'. The chords change on every beat (i.e. every other quaver melody note). We start with a little bit of contrary motion, i.e. melody rising and bass note falling. Keep it in the back of your mind that the bass line descends to E and then returns to C before the final cycle sequence of D7/A G7 . Notice how we only briefly move away from a C chord before returning to it. Altogether you have the contributory and interrelated points of:

(a) a bass movement in small intervals,
(b) a chord sequence (interrelated with the bass) that sticks closely to C on the cycle of fifths, and
(c) the development of your 'ear' which comes only with practice and repetition.

It is worth persevering with the intro since it consolidates the contribution of the bass note to the 'flow' of the music and hence will make your minds aware of, and your memories receptive to, further tunes containing similar principles.

This arrangement of THE LONDONDERRY AIR is simply an extension of all the principles and 'sounds' we meet in its introduction. You now have the approach and the ability to memorise the sequence, taking due note of the significance of each indicated bass note. When you strip the bass note detail away, the bones you are left with are simply chords adhering closely to the tonic C on the cycle of fifths. Revert back to the written chords with all the appropriate bass notes indicated and the 'flavour' and poignancy of this tune returns.

MEMORY JOGGERS	
ORGANISATION OF SECTIONS	
REPETITION (sections/lines melody/sequence)	
MATCHING CHORDS TO MELODY NOTES	
"RECOGNITION" NOTES	
"RECOGNITION" CHORDS	
FINGERING	
LYRICS	
"HEARING" THE SOUND	√
ASSOCIATION WITH OTHER SONGS	√

When the amount of harmonic information is increased, your chances of successfully memorising the tune are reduced, and unless we approach this piece from many different angles the job of understanding would be impossible.

Without playing a note, you can see the 'mechanical' link-up - small bass movement, chords sticking closely to the cycle, etc. but it is the 'sound' of these chords that you must memorise. You must know what sound to expect before you play it and this only comes through practice and familiarity. Taking the intro, for example, we remember the 'sound' F to F° from I LOVE YOU BECAUSE, and we remember from THE ANNIVERSARY WALTZ that when we add the augmented fifth (+) we promote a more unstable chord (e.g. C/E or C7+/E, leading to F). We remember from THE ENTERTAINER the sound of C/E and C/G and we saw Dm7/G G7 C back in I COULD HAVE DANCED ALL NIGHT.

24. Sunny

Words and Music
by Bobby Hebb

Sun - ny — yesterday my life was filled with rain.

Sun - ny — you smiled at me and real-ly eased the pain. Oh the

dark days are done and the bright days are here my Sunny one shines so sin-cere, Oh

Sun-ny one so true — I love you.—

SUGGESTED CHORD INVERSIONS										
F7	F A C E♭		Fmaj7	F A C E		Fm(maj7)	F A♭ C E		C7	G B♭ C E
Am	A C E	Am6	F♯ A C E	Am7	G A C E	E7	G♯ B D E	Bm7⁻⁵		F A B D

Not every tune lends itself to a 16's beat or disco interpretation, so in this instance we are able to develop our memories progressively with a tune that would fit the bill should we exhaust our sheet music and the disco dancers are insisting on more! In SUNNY we can relax from the mental rigours of THE LONDONDERRY AIR whilst still adding more basic ideas to our memories.

STRUCTURE				
WRITTEN KEY	STARTING/LEAD-IN NOTE CHORD		TEMPO/RHYTHM	ORGANISATION OF SECTIONS
C (Am)	E	Am	C=⁴/₄ DISCO ♩ 120	A B

It consists of just two 8 bar Sections A and B and has a minor flavour throughout – Am, written in the key of its relative major, C major.

HARMONIC PRINCIPLES ILLUSTRATED			
CYCLE OF FIFTHS	SIGNIFICANT BASS MOVEMENT	MOVING INTERNAL HARMONY	CHANGE OF TONALITY
√	√		

Sun-E, just notice how each small melodic phrase constantly reiterates the note of E, and with this predominant melody note in mind, you'll see how the harmonies in essence are simply Am and its preceding E7, encompassing a sequence of passing chords between Am and E7 founded upon a descending bass line.

Looking first at Section A, we notice that the foundation of the harmonic movement is the descending bass A G F & E. The harmonies follow this movement but the second chord is not an actual G chord but a compatible chord, C7, suspended over a G pedal – an important distinction. With the repeat of this harmonic movement in Section A, we reach Section B, based on similar principles but harmonically more interesting.

We first saw the principle of descending harmonies in GENTLE ON MY MIND, | C | Cmaj7 | C6 | , and we now couple this internal harmonic descent with a bass descent. The overriding descent is a pedal sequence of A G F with the inclusion of an F♯ pedal and a change of harmony above the F pedal (Fmaj7 to Fm[maj7]). Play this harmonic sequence on its own | Am | Am7/G | Am6/F♯ | Fmaj7 | Fm(maj7) | and once you have remembered the 'sound' of this sequence, fit it to the repetitive right hand melody 'motif' of notes E D C. Just to get our priorities sorted out: the melody is simple and the chords follow the pedal so we recognise immediately that the most important aspect is the bass progression.

The final line of Section B is simply the two points on the cycle preceding A, that is B & E (remember the sequence is contained within the word BEAD) and it's our old friend from EL CUMBANCHERO – | Dm7⁻⁵ | G7 | Cm | , equivalent here to | Bm7⁻⁵ | E7 | Am | .

MEMORY JOGGERS	
ORGANISATION OF SECTIONS	
REPETITION (sections/lines melody/sequence)	
MATCHING CHORDS TO MELODY NOTES	√
"RECOGNITION" NOTES	
"RECOGNITION" CHORDS	
FINGERING	
LYRICS	
"HEARING" THE SOUND	
ASSOCIATION WITH OTHER SONGS	√

Sun-E. Play the tune using whichever rhythm you like and remember the repeated use of the melody note of E. We also remember that the tune is based on Am and its dominant seventh, E7, with two interesting descending bass lines linking these two chords. We remember the bass first and then our memories select the chords to superimpose on it, although in practice we don't search too hard as, with familiarity, we recall that Section A contains a C7/G and Section B has the Am chord changing form to be compatible with the bass, i.e. | Am | Am7/G | Am6/F♯ | .

Finally, our knowledge of EL CUMBANCHERO, also written with a minor flavour, prompts us to remember the standard approach chords to the minor – | Bm7⁻⁵ | E7 | Am | .

One of the attractive features of SUNNY, from a player's point of view, is that it can be played in quite a leisurely fashion whilst the rhythm box (or drummer) is 'busy'.

25. Georgia On My Mind

Words by Stuart Gorrell

Music by Hoagy Carmichael

Bb7	F Ab Bb D	F	F A C	Fm6	F Ab C D	C7	G Bb C E	C7	E Bb C
C7+	E G# Bb C	G7	F G B D	Gm	G Bb D	Gm-5	G Bb Db		
Gm7	F G Bb D	Dm	F A D	A7	G A C# E	Am	A C E		
Am7	G A C E	E7	G# B D E	Em7	G B D E	F#°	F# A C D#		

STRUCTURE				
WRITTEN KEY	STARTING/LEAD-IN		TEMPO/RHYTHM	ORGANISATION OF SECTIONS
	NOTE	CHORD		
F	A	F	4/4 SWING ♩ 84	A₁ A₂B A₃

Note the similarities between A_1, A_2 & A_3 and observe the minor tonality of the Middle Eight Section B.

HARMONIC PRINCIPLES ILLUSTRATED

CYCLE OF FIFTHS	SIGNIFICANT BASS MOVEMENT	MOVING INTERNAL HARMONY	CHANGE OF TONALITY
√	√		√

Do you remember the 'Blackpool Tower' sequence | F | A7 | Dm | which, essentially, was F to its relative minor, Dm, via one stop on the cycle? Now we slip in an extra chord of Em7 just to effect a smooth transition and to get you ready for our next example, YESTERDAY, where we really do 'dwell' on this sequence. For now, just play and enjoy the 'sound' of | F | Em7 | A7 | Dm | and remember it as an extension of the 'Blackpool Tower' sequence. Notice how we can split up and overlap the sequences in Section A₁ | F | Em7 | A7 | Dm | + | Dm | Gm | | F | E7 | | Gm7 | C7 | F | | F | F#° | Gm7 | C7+ | - a series of mini-sequences that your memories will soon recognise and 'hear'. Let's look at them individually:

| F | Em7 | A7 | Dm | - a smoother transition to the relative minor than the more abrupt | F | A7 | Dm | .

| Dm | Gm | - simply a cycle movement (but excluding the C7 and returning to F directly).

| F | E7 | - a semitone bass movement for effect/drama as we first saw in SHOW ME THE WAY TO GO HOME.

| Gm7 | C7 | F | - a basic cycle sequence.

| F | F#° | Gm7 | C7+ | - our old friend from THE ANNIVERSARY WALTZ, returning to the clockwise part of the cycle.

How about the Middle Eight where the tonality changes to Dm? Simply three repeated cycle movements, | Dm | Gm | Dm | each time moving on to a chord compatible with the melody note but introducing a different flavour to the end of each phrase, chords of Bb7, G7, E7 respectively. Just as we remember, in SUNNY, the principle of the chords following the descending bass line, so we meet this idea again in the final phrase of Section B - bass notes of A G F# F & E before we play a blunt dominant seventh (C7) that immediately aligns our thinking back to the major tonality of F for the start of Section A₃. Although we may use the memory jogger of matching chords to the outside parameters of melody and bass notes, we do have a variety of choices open to us. In the same way that we remember a sequence of melody notes, we must try to remember a sequence of harmony 'sounds'.

MEMORY JOGGERS	
ORGANISATION OF SECTIONS	
REPETITION (sections/lines melody/sequence)	
MATCHING CHORDS TO MELODY NOTES	√
"RECOGNITION" NOTES	√
"RECOGNITION" CHORDS	
FINGERING	
LYRICS	
"HEARING" THE SOUND	√
ASSOCIATION WITH OTHER SONGS	√

A combination of new principles and cross references to earlier examples are the 'hooks' that pull an accurate recall from our memories. Break Section A₁ into manageable harmonic building blocks | F | Em | A7 | Dm | | Dm | Gm | | F | E7 | | Gm7 | C7 | F | | F | F#° | Gm7 | C7+ | and similarly Section B | Dm | Gm | Dm | times 3, plus the descending bass sequence.

The melody is smooth and flowing, and in the same manner that we remember SUNNY as revolving round an E note, so GEORGIA revolves round the 'third' note – A (the major third) in the major F section, and F (a minor third) in the Dm section.

26. Yesterday

Words and Music
by John Lennon & Paul McCartney

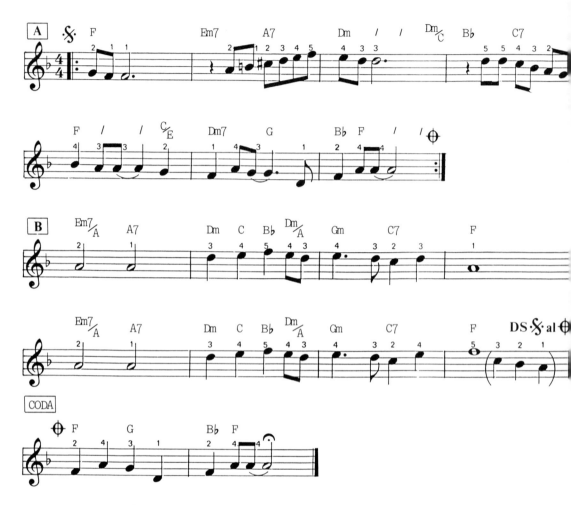

SUGGESTED CHORD INVERSIONS							
Bb	F Bb D	F	F A C	C	G C E	C7	E Bb C	G	G B D
Gm	G Bb D	Dm	F A D	Dm7	F A C D	A7	G A C# E	Em7	G B D E

The flavour of songwriting changed considerably in the 1960's, largely due to the prolific pens of John Lennon and Paul McCartney, and so YESTERDAY is an excellent example of a familiar and well-loved song from that era for our memories to store.

STRUCTURE				
WRITTEN KEY	STARTING/LEAD-IN NOTE	CHORD	TEMPO/RHYTHM	ORGANISATION OF SECTIONS
F	G	F	4/4 ROCK ♩ 96	A B

When we memorised GENTLE ON MY MIND, we needed a nudge to remember those extra 2 bar passages, but when a tune meanders through the harmonies as in YESTERDAY, we tend to lose sight of the fact that Section A is a shorter, non-standard, 7 bar sequence – not that it matters because our memories follow the melody without retaining the overall sense of 4 and 8 bar patterns that comes with the repetition of individual melodic phrases. The written key is F, but notice how scarcely a melodic phrase goes by without reference to Dm, the relative minor of F.

HARMONIC PRINCIPLES ILLUSTRATED			
CYCLE OF FIFTHS	SIGNIFICANT BASS MOVEMENT	MOVING INTERNAL HARMONY	CHANGE OF TONALITY
√	√		√

In our last example, GEORGIA ON MY MIND, we met the sequence $\boxed{F\ Em7\ A7\ Dm}$ for the first time and we now consolidate our appreciation of this 'sound' by reference to its application in YESTERDAY. Just as we listened to a displace- ment from the tonic in LOVE ME TENDER $\boxed{G\ A7}$ where the root note of the harmony moved up a tone, we compare this with the 'sound' (which must be practised and stored in your memory) of the pedal descending a semitone. Now play and compare the same type of sequence $\boxed{F\ Em7\ A7\ Dm}$ in:

TITLE	WRITTEN KEY	SEQUENCE IN WRITTEN KEY
IT'S IMPOSSIBLE	G	G F#m7^{-5} B7 Em
IF I RULED THE WORLD	E♭	E♭ Dm7 G7 Cm
BE MY LOVE	G	G F#m7^{-5} B7 Em

Such is its importance that we must remember it in YESTERDAY and then our memories will reproduce it for us whenever we 'hear' that it is called for – yet another sequence now in our memory libraries.

Notice how we link up the pedal notes to make small bass sequences and how the chords are notated to follow suit. Again, as in THE NATIONAL ANTHEM, it isn't the pedal following the chord, it's the chord following the pedal! Overall the harmonies follow the cycle of fifths, B♭ F C G D roots in the major phrases, and Dm, with preceding chords based on roots of A & E, in the minor phrases. Having established, visually, the chords you will play, the next job is to memorise the 'sounds' of major and minor and the approach to each, i.e. $\boxed{Gm\ C7\ F}$ or $\boxed{B♭\ F}$ if major or $\boxed{Em7\ A7\ Dm}$ if minor, and then start to help your memory by developing the idea of displacement from the tonic. We already recognise the sound of F to G7 (the same relative movement as in LOVE ME TENDER) and now we can recognise the sound of the sequence $\boxed{F\ Em7\ A7\ Dm}$. We also have to distinguish between returning to F from C7, or from B♭, which consolidates the work done at the start of the BASIC SECTION in HAPPY BIRTHDAY TO YOU.

MEMORY JOGGERS	
ORGANISATION OF SECTIONS	
REPETITION (sections/lines melody/sequence)	
MATCHING CHORDS TO MELODY NOTES	√
"RECOGNITION" NOTES	
"RECOGNITION" CHORDS	
FINGERING	
LYRICS	
"HEARING" THE SOUND	√
ASSOCIATION WITH OTHER SONGS	√

Start positively and remember $\boxed{F\ Em7\ A7\ Dm}$ from whichever example is most familiar to you. Once again we can match melody notes to chords in bar 2 – B natural with Em7 and C# with A7, etc. The lyrics are sad – all his troubles are here to stay – so the brighter sound of the major gives way to the melancholy 'flavour' of the minor. When we have established this flavour, we remember the 'passing' chords that follow the 'link-up' bass notes, e.g. $\boxed{Dm\ C\ B♭}$ $\boxed{F\ C/E\ Dm7}$ etc. Once again, this is a deceptive tune to memorise, but one full of interesting musical principles and so well worth the effort. Don't simplify the pedals/bass notes, or omit chords, since these are the most rewarding aspects. It takes a long time to assimilate all this information into your memory and reproduce it simultaneously, but practise it section by section and it will repay your efforts of will and self-discipline.

27. The Dam Busters March

Music by Eric Coates

SUGGESTED CHORD INVERSIONS									
Ab°	Ab B D F		F	F A C		C	G C E	C7	G Bb C E
Cm	G C Eb	G		G B D	G+	G B D♯	G7	F G B D	D7	F♯ A C D
Dm	F A D	Dm7		F A C D	Dm7⁻⁵	F Ab C D	A	A C♯ E	Am	A C E
Am7	G A C E	E		G♯ B E	Em	G B E	Em7	G B D E	C♯°	G Bb C♯ E

To be played 'con spirito' – with gusto. A perfect tune to enable the organist to display both the organ's versatility and his own prowess, and therefore an essential piece for the final category in the ADVANCED SECTION.

STRUCTURE				
WRITTEN KEY	STARTING/LEAD-IN		TEMPO/RHYTHM	ORGANISATION OF SECTIONS
	NOTE	CHORD		
C	G	C/G	2/4 MARCH ♩ 132	Intro. A B etc.

This tune is evenly constructed of a 16 bar introduction plus a series of 16 bar sections, of which we have only sufficient space to consider the first two. There are two crotchet beats per bar (2/4), so make sure you practise and gradually work the tempo up to a spirited ♩ = 132, 2/4 pulse.

HARMONIC PRINCIPLES ILLUSTRATED			
CYCLE OF FIFTHS	SIGNIFICANT BASS MOVEMENT	MOVING INTERNAL HARMONY	CHANGE OF TONALITY
√	√	√	√

Let's start by considering the pedals again, and this time the aspect of what to do if there isn't a specific pedal instruction. The 2/4 feel necessarily means 2 pedals per bar, but when we reach Sections A and B, which pedals do we use for the alternate beat? In the absence of a specific instruction (after our memories have easily remembered the sustained 'pedal' bass of the intro), we play root and fifth, but we must call on our knowledge of chord construction to anticipate any possible 'clashes'. Note the Cm/A in line 3 of Section A and the Dm7-⁵ in line 2 of Section B where a root and fifth treatment of bass notes A to E and D to A respectively, would clash with the component harmony notes of E♭ and A♭. In these instances, keep your pedals firmly on the indicated root (and so play two A's and two D's).

INTRO

Let's think back to the mechanical basis of our very first example where we simply moved our triad 'shape' up and down on the keyboard, and we can see that we may also do this in the introduction to THE DAM BUSTERS MARCH. Keep your triad shape fixed and move it steadily up the keyboard from the C triad, whilst maintaining a constant G bass. Soon your memory will predict what type of 'sound' you will achieve when you move your chords in this fashion, and you may extend this sense of experiment to tunes such as THE SPANISH GIPSY DANCE, EVERGREEN, etc. 'Pedal' bass then becomes a harmonic 'device' that is firmly memorised for both its principle and the modern variety of sound that it can promote. Don't forget the interpretation. When you see dots over the notes, play them in staccato fashion and when you see a mixture of signs, slurs and staccato for example, make sure you adhere to the composer's instructions. After the staccato lead-in phrases (line 4) of the intro, we approach the first 16 bar Section A.

SECTION A

We have a fascinating mix of principles: the cycle, pedal progressions and even a brief implied change of tonality. Taking the significant pedal movement first, line 1 possesses a typical 'ragtime' descending pedal movement of the type we first memorised in THE ENTERTAINER providing (a) additional harmonic interest, (b) a bridge between lines 1 & 2, (c) a 'foil' to the emphasised melody note of E. Line 4's pedal movement is even more interesting as it closely ressembles the one we memorised in THE ANNIVERSARY WALTZ, but in this tune we use the sequence to pull us back to our written key of C, having strayed to an implied tonality of G at the start of line 4.

Once we (1) look at the chords, (2) listen to their sounds and the different ways they could lead our ears, (3) prepare our minds and memories to be receptive to sudden changes of direction, we understand and memorise from more than one approach. Our ears are comforted by multiples of 4 bar patterns, and when we get to bar 11 we can see we could easily finish the composition ourselves by extending the chord of C to bar 12 and then, with very little change to the melody, compose the last 4 bars around the chords of
| A7 | D7 | Dm7 | G7 | . But no, it isn't to be, and we are now receptive to the tonality change to G and our minds and ears anticipate it. We are now receptive to chords that 'bridge the gap' so look at that lovely chord Cm/A in bar 12 which has a foot on both sides of the bridge: Cm on one side, but the A pedal changes it to a chord that could also precede a tonality of G on the cycle - a sparser version of Am7-⁵. Just as we missed out the most immediate approach chord in GEORGIA ON MY MIND (Dm Gm → F), so that A pedal and the melody notes of G & A cross us over the bridge from C to G before the final 2 bars of Section A where the G7 chord anticipates a return to C. We could indeed stay just on G7, but the ascending pedals contained within | G7 | C♯° | G7/D | G7 | provide interest and a sense of resolution into the next section of this march.

Yet again, throughout this section, the significance of the bass movement is of paramount importance. We have moved away from the earlier concept that we memorise just melody line and chords. The correct order of priority is melody line, bass line and then chords! Do you remember in Section A where we observed the ambiguous use of Cm/A, a chord with an application in tonalities of both C and G? How about Dm7^{-5} for an interesting chord? Notes of D F A$\flat$ C could lead our inquisitive minds to consider it as Fm6/D or even a chord that precedes C on the cycle (via the G7 if appropriate). But what if our memories are not quite convinced about its 'dual nationality', belonging to both F and C tonalities? Dm7^{-5} (D F A$\flat$ C) may be called the 'split' or 'half' diminished chord (not quite the D F A$\flat$ B of the 'full' diminished). We know that the full diminished doesn't have a tonality of its own, thus permitting it to be used in bridging applications. Similarly, the 'split' diminished chord, the minor seventh with the flattened fifth (m7^{-5}) can also be used as a 'bridging' chord if appropriate, or as an approach chord to the tonality lying two points further round the cycle (as seen in EL CUMBANCHERO $\boxed{\text{Dm7}^{-5} | \text{G7} | \text{Cm}}$). We see the split diminished's big brother, the full diminished, in the form of A$\flat$° in line 3 and we observe chords from the cycle, one degree anti-clockwise and up to 4 degrees clockwise (roots of F C G D A E). When the pedals aren't 'root and fifth', the alternative is as notated, constituting small movements, with chords following this more important bass note sequence.

MEMORY JOGGERS	
ORGANISATION OF SECTIONS	
REPETITION (sections/lines melody/sequence)	
MATCHING CHORDS TO MELODY NOTES	
"RECOGNITION" NOTES	
"RECOGNITION" CHORDS	
FINGERING	√
LYRICS	
"HEARING" THE SOUND	√
ASSOCIATION WITH OTHER SONGS	√

As regards the right hand, you must observe and remember the interpretation marks – slurs, staccato signs and the full value sign (-) which gives the note its full time value. As regards bass notes, play root and fifth provided the fifth is compatible. (N.B. not on m7^{-5} chords) unless there is a more significant bass sequence as a moving foundation for the harmonies. Your memory of the dynamics will assist your recall of the precise notes that need to be played.

As regards the left hand, memorise the chords indicated and don't add sixths and sevenths if none are called for since they only introduce flavours that are not intended. Memory and practice will make your left hand move fluently and accurately, but first you must play from the copy to memorise the intended 'sound' of each chord.

After Section B, the tune progresses to Section C which has a tonality of F, but such is the length of THE DAM BUSTERS MARCH that you are referred to the sheet music should your appetite be whetted by your memory and interpretation of the first two sections.

28. Air On The G String

by J.S. Bach

SUGGESTED CHORD INVERSIONS								
F	F A C	C	G C E	C7	G B♭ C E	G	G B D	G7	F G B D
D7	F♯ A C D	Dm	F A D	A	A C♯ E	A7	G A C♯ E
A7−9	G B♭ C♯ E	Am	A C E	Am7	G A C E	E7	G♯ B D E
E7−9	F G♯ B D	Em7−5	G B♭ D E	E°	G B♭ C♯ E	Bm7−5	F A B D

Air on the G String

This piece is included to enable the seriously minded home organ student to progress into a more classical field, having once learned to play the organ via the 'popular' presentation of music in melody line and chord symbol form. Necessarily our arrangement here must be acceptable to all persuasions, carrying enough information in an easy-to-read format without losing any essential 'flavour'. So that the chord symbols may be left relatively uncluttered, the bass instruction is omitted from them and written in full in bass clef.

STRUCTURE				
WRITTEN KEY	STARTING/LEAD-IN		TEMPO/RHYTHM	ORGANISATION OF SECTIONS
	NOTE	CHORD		
C	E	C	$\frac{4}{4}$ ♩ 72	A B C

This piece is written in C, surprisingly enough (it is actually the second movement from Bach's Third Orchestral Suite in D rearranged as a violin solo in C), but does, through its three 12 bar sections, progress through tonalities of C G Am G and finally C.

HARMONIC PRINCIPLES ILLUSTRATED			
CYCLE OF FIFTHS	SIGNIFICANT BASS MOVEMENT	MOVING INTERNAL HARMONY	CHANGE OF TONALITY
√	√		√

We keep to logical subdivisions of 12 bar sections, but just as with YESTERDAY, we meander through the 'changes' (harmonic sequences) following a melodic line which doesn't help our sense of time displacement. (Compare our standard song studies in the BASIC and INTERMEDIATE SECTIONS which have repetitive melodies symmetrically contained within 8 or 12 bar frameworks.) Observe the interrelationship of the melody and bass line and first focus your memories on these 'outside' notes before playing the intervening harmonies. We've built towards this final classical example via stepping stones of THE NATIONAL ANTHEM and THE LONDONDERRY AIR, so let's now recall all the harmonic 'devices' we have already memorised and to which we may now cross refer:

(1) The movement of the bass in small, significant intervals.

(2) The compatibility of the harmony with the melody and bass notes.

(3) The overall conformity of the harmonies to the cycle of fifths, being founded upon chords in the clockwise part of the cycle and one degree anti-clockwise from the key chord.

(4) The relative absence of unstable harmonic components such as sevenths, thus giving the sparseness of harmony that is desired.

(5) The ambiguous use of chords such as diminisheds and 'split' diminisheds (E°, Em7^{-5}) which need not possess a tonality of their own and which 'bridge' between chords more directly related to the tonic (as we saw in THE DAM BUSTERS MARCH).

MEMORY JOGGERS	
ORGANISATION OF SECTIONS	
REPETITION (sections/lines melody/sequence)	
MATCHING CHORDS TO MELODY NOTES	√
"RECOGNITION" NOTES	
"RECOGNITION" CHORDS	
FINGERING	
LYRICS	
"HEARING" THE SOUND	√
ASSOCIATION WITH OTHER SONGS	√

Once we have built our memories via the preceding examples, AIR ON THE G STRING is a concentration of all the previous harmonic principles we have remembered. Before, in our early examples, we used to match our harmonies to our melody note to support our recall of the tune, but now we have to concentrate on the outside parameters of melody and bass and remember our harmony in relation to these two significant and essential notes.

Memory also consists of anticipation - we learn to anticipate what 'sound' we require next so, in addition to a 'visual' memory we have to develop, through practice and cross reference to other tunes, a 'sound' memory so that we can produce the sound we want to hear. The first thing our 'sound' memory does is to tell us when we're wrong! Thereafter it uses all the contributory factors of cross reference, visual recall and harmonic reasoning to keep us on the right road.

29.

Tico Tico

Music by Zequinha Abreu

Tico Tico

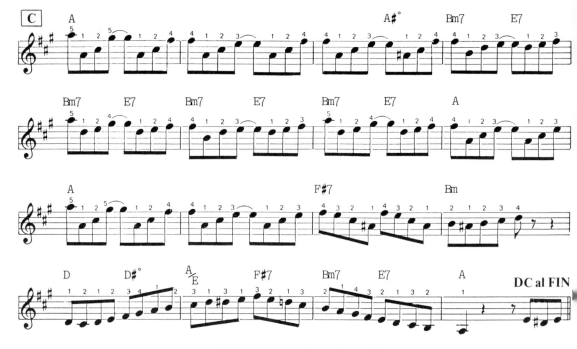

SUGGESTED CHORD INVERSIONS									
F	F A C	C	G C E	G7	F G B D	D	F♯ A D	Dm	F A D
Dm7	F A C D	A	A C♯ E	A7	G A C♯ E	Am		A C E	
E7	G♯ B D E	B7	F♯ A B D♯	Bm	F♯ B D	Bm7		F♯ A B D	
F♯7	F♯ A♯ C♯ E	F♯°	F♯ A C D♯	D♯°	F♯ A C D♯	A♯°		G A♯ C♯ E	

This is a samba that will always be associated with the organ because of its definitive interpretation by Ethel Smith. Your memory may rest easy on this piece because it consists almost entirely of ground you have covered in other examples – only the instruction BRIGHT SAMBA justifies its position as the final example in this book!

STRUCTURE				
WRITTEN KEY	STARTING/LEAD-IN NOTE	CHORD	TEMPO/RHYTHM	ORGANISATION OF SECTIONS
C	E	n/c	₵ SAMBA ♩ 116	A B C

The three 16 bar Sections A B & C each have a differing tonality, but can be easily memorised in relation to the first tonality of Am. The first change is to C (the relative major to Am) and the second change is to A major itself. The three lead-in notes are part of the tune, so a good idea for an introduction would be to play the final line of Section B, finishing on a C note which would precede in compatible fashion the opening chord of Am at the start of the tune.

HARMONIC PRINCIPLES ILLUSTRATED			
CYCLE OF FIFTHS	SIGNIFICANT BASS MOVEMENT	MOVING INTERNAL HARMONY	CHANGE OF TONALITY
√	√		√

Remember that no matter which tonality we are in, be it major or minor, the cycle of fifths rules apply equally, and so in Section A we encounter chords one degree anti-clockwise from Am (Dm) and chords up to two degrees clockwise (E7 & B7). Similarly, the bulk of Sections B and C are based upon the tonic chord and those chords that lie 2 degrees clockwise on the cycle. Once we pinpoint the tonality, therefore, the chords are easy to memorise until we reach the last lines of Sections B and C. The principle, which is identical for each, is a return to the tonic from one point anti-clockwise via that ever-useful diminished chord acting as a 'bridge'. $\boxed{F}\boxed{F\sharp^\circ}\boxed{C/G}$ gets us back to a C tonality whilst keeping faith with the principle of small bass movements, before we cast out once more and fill the final 2 bars with our now familiar cycle sequence. (Notice the parallel harmonic movement in line 4 of Section C where the harmonic sequence has been displaced by an interval of a minor third.)

MEMORY JOGGERS	
ORGANISATION OF SECTIONS	
REPETITION (sections/lines melody/sequence)	√
MATCHING CHORDS TO MELODY NOTES	√
"RECOGNITION" NOTES	
"RECOGNITION" CHORDS	
FINGERING	√
LYRICS	
"HEARING" THE SOUND	√
ASSOCIATION WITH OTHER SONGS	

You won't have time to stop and make measured choices of harmonies - when you are up to speed your memory will just guide your instinct. This instinct is based upon practice, repetition and familiarity and you don't have time to actually stop and remember. For this reason we need to remember TICO TICO in a familiar form where the chords are unwaveringly constant, giving our minds freedom to concentrate on our right hands which is where our problems will lie. Building up a right hand technique and adopting a consistent and logical fingering pattern are all important for memorising. The version of TICO TICO that we reproduce here is not at all easy as regards fingering, but to rearrange the bars that contain repetition on the same notes would be to avoid the issue. Such is the popularity of TICO TICO that if you cannot master the difficult sections at tempo, then there are several simpler arrangements available.

Repeating notes with the same finger only 'works' up to a certain tempo (depending on your finger agility), whereafter the sound degenerates into mistimed notes with consequent loss of rhythmic clarity. Try the suggested fingering and do not dismiss its apparent difficulty without first using it over the course of 2 or 3 practice sessions, and even then only change it if you have a method which suits you that avoids repeating the same fingers in succession. (The exception to this is in Section C where your fourth finger doubles up naturally.)

Next in importance to be remembered after the fingering is the 'sound' of the sequence in line 4 of Section B, bearing in mind that this is a passage that could be used as an intro. This demands a build-up of technique in the left hand and bass pedal department and is a candidate for 'practice makes perfect'. Just as we may always approach memory through the medium of understanding, so it is a truism that '...technique is half in the head and half in the hands'. The 'understanding' half is to appreciate that $\boxed{F}\boxed{F\sharp^\circ}\boxed{C/G}$ is a cycle return from one point anti-clockwise and $\boxed{A7}\boxed{Dm7}\boxed{G7}\boxed{C}$ is a self-contained cycle sequence to land us positively back on the tonic chord of C. Once you understand this, play the inversions shown and build your coordination between pedals and left hand before blending this with the 'sparkling' right hand passage. (The same principle applies to line 4 of Section C).

Just as we organise our music and our approach in order to memorise successfully, so in this instance we have to organise a 'pulse' in our music if the notes are not to be considered as a random jumble. The overriding 'pulse' is the two pedal beats per bar and we must 'phrase' our music with this in mind to give our performance 'shape' and 'form'. Notice how very often you have a quaver rest in the centre of the bar to enable this pulse to be distinctly heard, so emphasise the 'gap' and let your memory recall more than just harmony and melody details. As you build up speed in your practice, you can still retain the two beat 'pulse' without appearing laboured.

Relax now, the practical work is behind you to return to as you fancy, and all that remains is for you to consolidate all the aspects that have contributed to 'memory via understanding' so that you can apply them readily when you come to memorise fresh material.

TABULATION OF HARMONIC PRINCIPLES ILLUSTRATED IN ADVANCED SECTION

EXAMPLE	TITLE	HARMONIC PRINCIPLES ILLUSTRATED			
		CYCLE OF FIFTHS	SIGNIFICANT BASS MOVEMENT	MOVING INTERNAL HARMONY	CHANGE OF TONALITY
21	HEARTS AND FLOWERS	√	√		
22	THE NATIONAL ANTHEM	√	√		
23	THE LONDONDERRY AIR	√	√		
24	SUNNY	√	√		
25	GEORGIA ON MY MIND	√	√		√
26	YESTERDAY	√	√		√
27	THE DAM BUSTERS MARCH	√	√	√	√
28	AIR ON THE 'G' STRING	√	√		√
29	TICO TICO	√	√		√

I do hope you have found this book interesting and stimulating and that it will continue to add to your enjoyment of music. Remember –

The Key to Progress in Music is

MEMORY

HOW TO PLAY MUSIC BY EAR

DON'T SHOOT THE

ORGANIST